CLINICAL PSYCHOLOGY REFLECTIONS VOLUME 4

CONNOR WHITELEY

No part of this book may be reproduced in any form or by any electronic or mechanical means. Including information storage, and retrieval systems, without written permission from the author except for the use of brief quotations in a book review.

This book is NOT legal, professional, medical, financial or any type of official advice.

Any questions about the book, rights licensing, or to contact the author, please email connorwhiteley@connorwhiteley.net

Copyright © 2024 CONNOR WHITELEY

All rights reserved.

DEDICATION
Thank you to all my readers without you I couldn't do what I love.

INTRODUCTION

Clinical psychology is an amazing area of psychology. It can improve lives, transform them and save people for the better, and it can decrease psychological distress too. That's why I love this great area of psychology.

However, the problem with how clinical psychology is taught in lecture theatres and formal education is that there are only so many topics you can teach, only so many debates you can talk about and there is only so much research in the world so you cannot have lively, heated debates at university.

I wanted somewhere to address this issue.

Therefore, I decided to write these clinical psychology reflection books where I can use evidence and research and my own fact-based opinions to explore some of the hottest debates in clinical psychology. As well as explore other topics from a clinical psychology perspective.

All these books are extremely fun to write and

are fascinating so I know you're going to enjoy them as well. Also, this has to be the best book in the series so far, because it explores topics in a lot more depth and we tackle some truly thought-provoking topics that impact the highest levels of clinical psychology practice and research.

If you're looking for an engaging, fascinating and easy-to-understand book exploring the edges of clinical psychology as well as other topics that you would never be taught at university, then this is the book for you.

You won't regret buying this book.

Who Am I?

Personally, I always love to know who the author is of the nonfiction I read so I know the information is coming from a good source. In case you're like me, I'm Connor Whiteley, the internationally bestselling author of over 40 psychology books.

In addition, I am the host of *The Psychology World Podcast,* a weekly show exploring a new psychology topic each week and delivering the latest psychology news. Available on all major podcast apps and YouTube.

Finally, I am a psychology graduate studying a Clinical Psychology Masters at the University of Kent, England.

So now we know more about each other, let's dive into some great clinical psychology reflections.

POVERTY FACTORS IN MENTAL HEALTH AND COST OF LIVING CRISIS

"People have to decide between heating homes and eating. That isn't good for mental health,"

- Paraphrased words of Dr Joshua Nice, Clinical Psychologist

Normally, whenever I start writing these clinical psychology reflection books, I always try to start off nice and easy. I try to start with interesting but not very challenging topics to lure in readers, but in this reflection book I am flat out not doing that.

Due to I'm writing this in 2023 and we're in the middle of a cost of living crisis but hopefully towards the end of it. Therefore, I'm sure you know that all the prices are going on, mortgages are increasing and disposable income is decreasing. I actually went to the shops earlier and four pints of milk now costs £2.50 so over 3 USD. I still remember when I was a child in the early 2000s when four pints of milk cost less than a pound or dollar for our international audience.

In addition, I know UK mortgage rates are decreasing but after the very interesting and non-political Mini-Budget done by the UK Government in late 2022, mortgages in the South East where I live went from 2% to 10% but now they are about 5%.

Anyway, as you can see everything is getting more expensive and I didn't even touch on how energy bills have increased 100s% over the past two years in the UK.

This is bad enough for everything but when we consider that out of all the factors that cause mental health conditions and difficulties to develop, poverty is the single factor we know the most about and it causes the most mental health difficulties.

Therefore, it sadly isn't surprising that mental health difficulties and conditions have only increased over the course of the COVID-19 pandemic and the global cost of living crisis meaning that mental health services are getting even more overwhelmed than they were pre-COVID.

The reason why I wanted to reflect on this is because there are three main areas we need to discuss so we can at least be aware of how this affects mental health, and how our current or future clients might feel. We need to reflect on the debate itself about whether a client should heat their home or eat, I want to reflect on poverty at both an individual level and then at a society level without getting political.

Firstly, if a client comes into the therapy room in the UK (where healthcare is thankfully free as of 2023 but who knows how much longer), then it's great that they don't have to pay for their mental health therapy. I know this is a major concern for other countries.

Yet if clients have depression, for example, because they're constantly worried or have Negative Automatic Thoughts surrounding their poverty and paying the bills. Then this is a massive societal-level factor causing or maintaining their depression.

And let's face it, this is very hard for all therapists to deal with. Especially if you're a Cognitive Behavioural Therapist because you can (sort of) only deal with a person's negative and biased cognitions about themselves, the world and others. You cannot help them with their poverty.

Unless you can.

Whilst I refuse to believe the whole debate between should a client should eat, pay for therapy or heat their homes is a debate that should exist in the first place, there is still a lot of clinical psychologists can do to help these people affected by poverty.

A clinical psychologist could recommend resources and support for the client to engage with to help them. Then this might help lessen the psychological distress caused by the poverty and living situation, and going forward this might help the client focus more on the therapy and have less evidence to confirm their Negative Automatic Thoughts.

That's why one point of this reflection is to help you realise that psychology will always be a powerful force for good, even if you're dealing with societal-level factors, therapies like CBT and the other cognitive waves of psychotherapy can still be a powerful force for good.

Also, in this situation you would possibly draw on other therapeutic models as well depending on what you're trained in and what would best meet the client's needs.

For example, just two random examples here, would be that systemic therapy might be needed if the client's difficulties around poverty has something to do with their partner's negative reaction to stress causing other issues in the family system. That's one example. Or narrative therapy concepts might be effective if the therapist felt the need to want to change the client's narrative around poverty and what it means about them as a person.

This is a useful idea that I'll reflect on later on getting creative in the concept of "therapy".

Then lastly, I want to reflect on poverty at an individual-level and societal level because this does have very important mental health implications.

Firstly, and this really connects to Negative Automatic Thoughts and beliefs about the self, if you're in poverty and you have a family that you cannot feed, heat and go to therapy. Then you will feel like a failure of a parent, you will feel immensely guilty and worse because you're in a situation that ultimately isn't your fault.

Yet because you feel guilty, sad and a failure then

you will probably start to develop a mental health condition, like depression or anxiety or something else depending on other factors.

My point is poverty does a lot of damage and harm to innocent people that are struggling and that's why therapists are so important. Since despite what various rich people believe, people rarely make decisions that make them end up in poverty. Most of the time, it is societal, generational and other social inequalities that make people end up or continue a cycle of poverty.

If you doubt me or are interested then definitely look into the research on those reasons because it is really interesting.

This is why, at a societal level, it's so important that we focus on reducing poverty, helping innocent people and stopping the worse mental health outcomes from happening to these people.

The United Nations and other groups are firm in wiping out poverty as it is in their Global Development Goals and I agree with them. For the sake of our mental health and the mental health of the most vulnerable in society, we need to take very firm action against poverty.

No one should be in poverty so let's start walking towards a future where poverty is a thing of the past. We can all donate a tiny amount of money to a charity, we can donate to a food bank and we can all make sure our friends and family members are okay.

Those are just some of the simple things we can

do to create a better future for everyone in society no matter how poor they are. And maybe, just maybe this will be the difference between them developing a mental health condition and them not.

WHY THERE NEEDS TO BE MORE SUPPORT FOR RESEARCHERS?

Personally, I am absolutely fascinated by our next reflection because I forget the academic paper on Incel and misogamy research I was reading, but there was a single line or comment that hooked me. It is the fact that there isn't enough support for researchers.

Now I completely agree with this and I do need to give a trigger warning before I give you more details.

<u>Trigger Warning</u>

The following reflection will refer to Incel and misogamy ideology and how these far-right groups want to legalise rape, beatings and violence against women.

Please do not continue reading if this is a triggering topic for you and PLEASE make sure you look after yourself if anything in this reflection is emotionally distressing for you. Talk to someone or talk to a mental health charity.

Back To The Reflection

The reason why I completely agree that there needs to be more mental health support for researchers is because when you're researching topics like Incel and misogamy and far-right ideology, you're going to go across from messed-up stuff.

The month before this is published in April 2024, I have my Applied Psychology book being published and a large section of that book is dedicated to the psychological theories and interventions applied to Incel and misogamy ideology.

I feel so sorry for these Incel researchers because they have to hear first hand how young and older men truly belief that women are evil, plotting, scheming bitches that are ruling the world and are actively plotting against men, and they're sole focus is enslaving men to do their evil, twisted bidding.

Of course that is complete rubbish.

Yet if you then add in the fact that these researchers have to listen to these people advocating in person or online that women need to be raped, beaten and killed for the safety of the male future. As well as how these idiots create memes to spread their hate and outrageous beliefs online, then this is a hell of a lot to handle.

I found it distressing and I was only reading the research and writing chapters of my book, I wasn't the one researching it first hand.

Just imagine about depressing, upsetting and angry that would make you have to research every single day of your working life, and you were constantly exposed to the darkness corners of humanity.

That would kill your mental health overtime. Even more so if you were a female researcher.

That's why it is absolutely critical that there is more mental health support put in place for academic researchers, because to the best of my knowledge, there isn't any. I suppose there might be some at certain universities but if my lecturers had a mental health crisis then I have no clue who they would turn too.

I suppose there's always the university's mental health resources, but not to be too dismissive, they are honestly useless in this situation. How the hell would a counsellor (not a fully trained clinical psychologist because in my experience they don't work at universities) that are used to working with students possibly help a researcher seeing such graphic stuff online.

I honestly doubt they would be much help, and that isn't a criticism of them personally. I've heard from tons of students that university mental health support teams are brilliant for *students* but Incel and misogamy researchers, I doubt it.

Therefore, I do strongly believe that we need to create mental health resources and teams for researchers. These may come in the form of other researchers on similar topics, just like how clinical psychologists have meetings with other clinical psychologists to make sure everyone's mental health is okay.

Yet there are problems with this approach.

The problem with reporting or talking to other researchers is the simple fact there's a chance the researcher you're talking to might steal your idea, research or data if you reveal that to them. Hence, the researcher needing support will not be able to talk freely out of want to protect their career to this other researcher and this will greatly limit the effectiveness of this approach.

I suppose universities could create specialist teams employing people that used to belong to these extremist communities as mental health supporters. This might be a cheaper option for the university as these people aren't highly trained professionals, like clinical psychologists, and because these people have gone through the whole Incel ideology process they can relate to the researchers.

Although, I suppose you could debate two main things. Firstly, do these people actually have any experience, training or useful resources to support researchers if they develop a form of PTSD, anxiety or depression because of the research material?

The answer is no.

Secondly, you could easily argue that if a researcher is feeling down, depressed and annoyed by something they see or hear in their Incel research, would they really want to talk to a former Incel member?

I'm not sure. Maybe. Maybe not.

Furthermore, you could have clinical psychologists with some kind of research background or practical experience with this sort of topic. This is the ideal goal I think because you have the clinical expertise, you have the knowledge about Incels or whatever extreme group they're researching and you have the academic background. So the clinical psychologist would be aware of the annoying university politics that could be playing a factor too in the researcher's distress.

Then again, how many clinical psychologists in the world have had a past career or focus in academia and specialist in extremism research?

Not a lot.

Overall, I'll fully admit that whatever happens next in research, psychology and university. We absolutely have to make sure that our researchers are protected as well as there is good psychological support available to them regardless of their research area.

It is all well and good us focusing on extremism, negativity and disgusting ideology, but this is all for nothing if we lose are bright, amazing and passionate researchers in the first place.

More must always be done to support these amazing people.

WHY YOU NEED TO HAVE AN EXPERIMENTAL ATTITUDE IN YOUR DEGREE?

One of the things that I love about clinical psychology is that you truly hear some weird golden nuggets and it isn't until you come to write a reflection like this, or until you suddenly remember it that you realise just how brilliant it is.

I was in a clinical psychology lecture a while ago and I think it was on Brief Psychological Interventions when my lecturer mentioned something that I utterly loved, and I really wanted to explore it in these pages.

It was something along the lines of, *you need an experimental attitude in our job.*

And that single sentence was so fascinating to me that I want to reflect on it now in different ways. I want to reflect on it in the therapy sense (the way she actually intended) but also how having an experimental attitude is important in any stage of your psychology journey. Since I know a good chunk of you wonderful readers will be psychology students.

Why You Need An Experimental Attitude In Your Degree?

Whilst I'm talking about your undergraduate degree here, I cannot see why these points wouldn't apply in later degrees. Therefore, having an experimental attitude is so, so critical in your undergraduate degree because it really helps you make the most of it.

For example, you really need to have an experimental attitude when it comes to choosing the type of degree you actually want. In this context, I mean of course want a psychology degree, but if you're looking at a university that offers different types of psychology degrees. Then you need to ask yourself what type? Do you want a placement? A year abroad? A degree specialising in clinical or forensic psychology?

Those are just some of the psychology degrees that my university offered and if I didn't want to be experimental and open to new possibilities then I never would have been on my Clinical Psychology degree with a placement year.

And honestly, me being open to doing a more specialised degree has had a few benefits. Firstly, it has made me so much more knowledgeable about clinical psychology compared to people only taking clinical optional modules. Secondly, it has reaffirmed that I want clinical psychology to be my career path and thirdly, I have met a great lecturer that has given me a lot of opportunities that I never ever would have had otherwise.

Another reason why you need to be experimental in your degree is it allows you to pick optional modules that you love, and know what ones you hate.

I know I've written about this before but I had such a nightmare with my final year optional modules because I wanted to take certain mental health ones, they didn't let me so I was stuck with a module called Cognition in Action.

Now I have no problem with cognitive psychology as you'll see later on in the book, but oh the heavens did I not want to do advanced cognitive psychology. But I had to.

Then the other optional module that I was allowed to pick was a mental health one that had been moved from Third Year to Second Year, but because this module was promised to us in First Year as a Third year one they were allowing us to take it.

I heard a lot of people not interested in doing a module with the Second Years but I didn't care. I just wanted the information and to learn.

Furthermore, I was rather "upset" in my final year that I wasn't allowed to take an optional module in Entertainment Law because I know a lot about that, I love the topic and I have a heavy interest in that topic. But I wasn't allowed to take it sadly and even now I haven't forgive the university. Evil people.

Moreover, a little note on finding a Final Year

Project or dissertation, you would have imagined me because my interest is in clinical psychology, I would have taken a clinical Project. But I didn't because I wanted to stay with my Placement Supervisor and work with him on his projects.

And I don't regret it for a single second.

Since he's a cognitive researcher by trade and I had said to him openly, I would never ever work on a cognitive project, I thought to myself that I was firm in that opinion. It turned out that I wasn't and I wasn't as closed off to the idea of cognitive psychology as I thought.

As well as when it comes to your degree being closed off to any idea, any topic, any opportunity, I think it is fatal mistake.

You're only at university for three years of your life and they honestly do go so fast, so please don't waste them, don't miss out on opportunities and enjoy it.

There have been a few opportunities in my first and second year that I do regret not taking because they would have helped me and made me get even more out of my degree. But then again, I wouldn't change anything about my life so you really need to see what's right for *your* situation and the degree that you want.

Overall, when it comes to choosing your optional modules and your final year project, you need to be experimental. Don't limit yourself to only doing certain things because it seems the "right" choice. If a module or project sounds interesting then check it out.

I always, always say that university is a time to experiment and look at different options. I never would do a cognitive psychology Final Year Project outside of university, so I wanted to have fun with my supervisor and continue to work with him, so I took a chance. I don't regret it. I took a chance with the type of degree I was going, and I seriously don't regret it.

Just go into your degree or go back into your degree mind (if you're already doing one) after reading this with an experimental attitude because you'll be amazed at what you discover.

And because this turned out to be a longer reflection than I intended, let's look at how having an experimental attitude benefits you in a psychotherapy sense.

WHY YOU NEED AN EXPERIMENTAL ATTITUDE IN PSYCHOTHERAPY?

I was rather surprised the length of the last reflection but I still know that it was filled with useful and interesting points, and this one will be no different.

Since when it comes to psychotherapy, whether you're a clinical psychologist now or in the future, you will always encounter different people with different mental health difficulties with different needs.

When I talk about needs, I mean they will have different maintaining factors and emotional or psychological needs that will make you need to change your approach to treatment. This shouldn't really come as a surprise given individual differences and the different information that goes into a formulation, but it all links to having an experimental attitude.

For example, if we take depression. If you look at the literature as a whole, listen to clinical psychologists as a whole and listen to clients as a whole then Cognitive Behavioural Therapy is the first point of call. And I have no problems at all with that because CBT is brilliant and it is really well supported in the literature.

However, Cognitive Behavioural Therapy just doesn't work for everyone and even in the good chunk of people that CBT does work for, there are different differences in treatment.

For instance, if we take two people with depression but they have two different major maintaining factors, and I know I am seriously oversimplifying the mental health conditions for writing and teaching purposes. Therefore, one person might have the main maintaining factor being they live in a very negative household and the other person might have a lot of toxic working relationships.

Both of these fictional examples show how standard CBT that is exactly the same for both people wouldn't work, because both people have different psychological needs to help them develop more adaptive coping mechanisms for *them* and *their* situation.

Hence, you need an experimental attitude in psychotherapy so you can realise that no two clients will ever have the same factors that can be solved by the exact same intervention. Every intervention needs to be adapted to the client but that is the point of formulation after all.

In addition, the main reason why you need an

experimental attitude builds upon the last point. Since if therapy you need to be experimental in your approach so you're open to exploring a wide range of possible interventions or parts of interventions to see what is best for your client.

For instance, at least in the UK, every psychotherapist is trained in 2 or more psychological therapies and this helps them to mix and match what they want to bring in with each client.

Some therapists are trained in cognitive behavioural therapy and narrative therapy or maybe systemic therapy. All these different therapies give you as a therapist different tools to use and pull out whenever you think it might be useful.

Personally, this is why I love integrative therapy. These are therapies that merge and combine different components from different therapies, because it gives therapists the freedom to explore and experiment with different therapies that will help their client.

And something I have touched in the past year and a bit is that in the clinical psychology literature, there is now a move towards understanding what individual components of different therapies are the most effective parts.

Due to cognitive behavioural therapy is amazing but if you look at the therapy when it's broken down into its different parts. The research shows that certain aspects, like behavioural activation if memory serves me right, is the most important aspect and the others are less so.

As a result without an experimental attitude a clinical psychologist would basically be tying one hand behind their back, because they would only be reading from the therapy manual, without even wanting to try and experiment with aspects or tools or techniques from other therapies that might help with their client's mental health difficulties.

I'll talk more about this in the next reflection but that's one of the great things about CBT. It gives you a great foundation that you can use to explore and experiment with other aspects as long as you keep using that CBT foundation.

I know one of my lecturers finds merging cognitive behavioural therapy with narrative therapy elements very useful. Since the basic idea of narrative therapy is people have narratives about themselves that are maladaptive and not helpful at all, so by rewriting these narratives and developing a new narrative about the client. This helps them to reduce their psychological distress.

This can work well with CBT if you think about it, because the basic idea of CBT is that it is our perceptions about events and beliefs that lead to mental health difficulties. Not the events themselves.

Therefore, CBT and narrative therapy can be merged together so the client can rewrite the narratives and cognitive beliefs they have about themselves. And I suppose (and don't quote me on this) but I think when you're explaining things to a client, I think talking about narratives and the personal "stories" we have about ourselves is certainly easier for them to understand. Compared to us talking about abstract mental processes, how these are negatively biased and we have faulty thinking patterns.

So I suppose there are other benefits to merging or at the very least using different forms of therapy to introduce concepts to clients.

Overall, clinical psychologists are scientists first and foremost and all scientists conduct experiments, ask questions and enjoy the process along the way. Therefore, maybe we all need to bring that playful, experimental attitude into the therapy room more so we can experiment with different models, concepts and tools so we can work out best how to help our client.

Not a single psychotherapy model has all the answers, but I truly believe that when we combine models then we are truly on the path to greatness. Each model targets something different so if we bring them together in a way that helps our client then we can cover a lot of interesting ground that ultimately decreases our client's psychological distress and improve their lives.

And if the key to those two things is having an experimental attitude then we absolutely have to do it, enjoy it and learn about it at the same time.

WHY STARTING WITH COGNITIVE BEHAVIOURAL THERAPY IS GOOD?

At least in the UK, because our healthcare is thankfully free at the time of writing, whenever a person with a mental health condition goes to the National Health Service, the only real opportunity (or at least the most common one) they have is Cognitive Behavioural Therapy. That's because it's effective, easy to implement and it doesn't "really" take as long as some of the other psychotherapies do. Like psychodynamic therapy and it is very much "one size fits all".

Making it cheap or cheaper than other therapies to deliver.

However, I know from a lot of service users and people in my clinical lectures who have been given therapy that it's annoying, because sometimes they don't need CBT, the need another form of psychotherapy but it isn't automatically offered.

Therefore, for the purpose of this reflection, I

want to focus in on the response to this point from my lecturer because I really like it, as well as it is certainly thought provoking. Because she said something along the lines of:

"CBT is good because it gives you a structure to follow and it gives you a foothold to use with clients,"

Personally, I completely understand that and this is the rather good thing about manualised psychotherapies because they do provide clinical psychologists with a lot of structure and then a therapist can apply their structure to the client to help them formulate.

Also, that's a great aspect about CBT, there are so many formulations and models that come with CBT that helps a clinical psychologist to understand the client better.

For instance, if we take the 5P model and focus on certain aspects for a moment. If a client comes in with a diagnosis of depression and they want to start treatment then this is perfect for CBT because their presenting factors and the other five Ps will really lent itself to the model. Hence, allowing the therapist to easily work with the client using this model to formulate an intervention.

But what if the client's representation isn't as straight forward?

Let's say a clinical psychologist is working with a client with depression but they start presenting and tell the psychologist about their attachment styles, trauma and other life experiences that suggest they don't have textbook depression.

What would happen then?

This is only a fact-based fictional example then the client could have a Complex Emotional Need (or personality "disorder" if we're using dated language) and these models don't really lend themselves to Cognitive Behavioural Therapy very well.

Yet all isn't lost because the clinical psychologist can still use CBT as a basis for the intervention or the investigating of the client's mental health difficulties so they can understand more about the client's experiences, difficulties and what they want to achieve with therapy.

Because let's face it, CBT is very comprehensive and that is why it gives therapists such a good foothold.

For example, whatever you think of CBT as a whole I think we all have to admit that the 5P model is super useful when it comes to talking to clients and getting information out of them. I'm not particularly aware of another form of psychotherapy that makes it so easy to explain the factors and extract information related to these factors out of clients.

Since if we want to understand the client's presenting factors (the maladaptive coping mechanism's they're showing) therapists can use a hot-cross bun or another visible formulation explain it to them and ask them. The exact same happens for the other four factors: precipitating, perpetuating, predisposing and protective factors.

Then once a therapist has gotten all the information from the client then they can work with them using their clinical expertise to determine whether or not CBT is the best course of action for them. Yet CBT is very useful for starting and structuring the therapy work at first with the client before then maybe determining CBT isn't right for them.

Another benefit of CBT is its visual nature and this makes it very useful in psychoeducation, because charts, timelines and all the very visual formulations you can do are great ways to introduce psychological concepts to clients, even as soon as that assessment interview.

Especially when we consider what if we want to find how maintaining or perpetuating factors cause their mental health condition to continue, this is a weird concept at first. And it might be difficult for clients to understand how their pushy mother (maintaining factor) is related to grandad dying (precipitating factor). Hence using a visual CBT chart of some sort is a good way to explain this visually to a client.

That's how CBT is useful as a foothold and structure.

However, I do understand that this is annoying for service users in the UK because they might have already researched the best form of therapy for people with their condition. Therefore, the fact that they have to go through a long, boring process of starting with another therapy is annoying and it hardly does anything good for motivation.

In this case, I think the solution to this is twofold and it requires something from both the client and the therapist as a whole.

Firstly, if a client is aware of the psychotherapy they actually need then the therapist needs to be open with them from the start. Either explaining that they will most probably get the form of therapy they want but it is easier and better for them to experience a little CBT first because of its structure and its other benefits, or the therapist explaining to the client that it is too expensive and it isn't offered by the NHS.

Secondly, when it comes to the client, as annoying as this is, they need to be patient and at least aware at a surface-level that clinical psychologists in the NHS are under immense amounts of pressure and they are seriously doing every single thing they can to help people. But it will never be enough and things aren't ideal.

That is sadly the way of the world but it doesn't mean the NHS and the clinical psychologists working in it aren't amazing.

Overall, CBT is brilliant and whilst there are problems with it, it is arguably the best therapy we have at the moment for a large range of conditions.

And even if CBT itself isn't useful for everyone, then its individual components definitely are and that is something that should excite everyone, therapist or not.

WHY YOU KNOW MORE THAN YOU THINK?

This is certainly a reflection that I've been wanting to write for a long, long time because it is so brilliant and useful for university students (and maybe professionals too) to know. Since at university, I think all students can back me up here but we are full of self-doubt and imposter syndrome.

Whilst we think this goes away after a while, and of course this self-doubt does decrease after our first year at university, it is still there and it can flare up at any moment.

I know that I was definitely filled with self-doubt during my final year last year because I was convinced that I would fail my exams and that my dissertation would be awful because I didn't know what I was talking about, but it turned out that I did do everything that I needed to do to succeed.

Therefore, I want to mention this for two reasons. A general reason and a clinical psychology reason, and I firmly believe that both reasons are critical things to reflect on.

Firstly, as university students, as long as you do the reading, go to your lecturers and try to be the best student you possibly can, whilst having fun at the same time. Then you will be a lot better off than other students, as well as if you're struggling then please seek out help at your university. For example, I know my university has the Student Learning Advisory service that is very useful at supporting students.

And you will be very pleasantly surprised at what you do and don't know about your topics when it comes to your dissertation, essays and other assignments. These are all scary things but once you get over the fear, anxiety and the self-doubt you'll realise that you are a lot better than you could ever hope to realise.

Then it is up to you to keep learning, asking for help when needed and hoping to improve your knowledge.

Additionally, whilst this isn't the big and important clinical psychology point I wanted to make, this will or could set you up very nice in the future because as a clinical psychology or another professional working within mental health, you will need to keep learning, exploring and developing your knowledge constantly in light of new literature and interventions.

If you can start to develop those skills now then

you'll be set up to develop them and use these valuable skills in the professional working environment.

How Does This Apply To Clinical Psychology?

This next part of the reflection is aimed at inspiring you, encouraging you and making you realise exactly how much extra knowledge you have about clinical psychology compared to other students.

The idea for this reflection actually came from a Prospectus Evening that I attended with some friends after a long day of testing on participants, and as much as the university wanted us to believe otherwise, this entire event was the university just marketing itself and wanting to keep us on.

They had a forensic psychologist, social psychologists, cognitive people and a bunch of clinical psychologists there, and after helping myself to the free pizza and catching up with my Final Year Project supervisor socially, I went back over to my friends to see they were talking to a lecturer of mine, a clinical psychologist.

And what really struck me were the questions they were asking. They weren't dumb questions, they weren't ignorant questions (well that ignorant) and they weren't questions that made me question why the hell they wanted to go into clinical psychology (well slightly). They were simply basic questions that they would have known the answers to if they had taken clinical psychology modules.

Now I am not disrespecting my friends because

they are great people, always up for a laugh and they're very supportive. But I was surprised that for people who have said repeatedly that they want to go into clinical psychology for a career, they haven't taken any "real" clinical psychology modules.

By "real", I mean at my university there are modules of the neuroscience of cognitive disorders and learning about people with learning disabilities. Granted they were modules that hadn't started when this Prospectus evening was, but those modules are still highly problematic, especially the first one.

The Neuroscience of Cognitive Disorders is a cognitive psychology module that looks at the neuroscience and theory behind a clinical psychology issue.

I have no problem whatsoever with the module itself because clinical psychology needs brilliant, amazing and intelligent cognitive people to work on clinical issues to help us understand them.

However, I cannot understand why people who want to work in clinical psychology don't choose clinical modules. Since this cognitive psychology module doesn't look at neurological assessments, how you would go about doing it, how the NHS works, what your job as a clinical psychologist would involve and all the millions of other clinical psychology concepts that I've written about in my books or spoken about on my podcast.

It is that real clinical psychology that students need. Students need to know how our profession works, the difficulties we face and the support that is available to them if they do decide to go into clinical psychology.

Because let's face it, you could be an expert in the cognitive theory of depression and dementia, but you would be next to useless if a person walks through the door to your therapy room and you have no idea what to do next.

Of course if the person lacked that knowledge completely they wouldn't get the job anyway.

But my point is that if you read clinical psychology books, listen to podcasts (like The Psychology World Podcast) and take clinical psychology modules at university then you are in such a better, stronger position compared to so many other people that *want* to be clinical psychologists.

If you're a person that does want to become a clinical psychologist but aren't doing these things yet, then I honestly don't mean to offend you. And to be honest, you're reading this book and that is a massive step in the right direction because the entire point of these reflections is to reflect on clinical psychology issues.

You'll learn something just by reading this.

Clinical psychology is an amazing journey but all journeys have to start somewhere and it is up to the people themselves when and how they start. But they have to start learning the ins and outs of clinical psychology at some point.

And personally, I think it should certainly be

sooner rather than later.
What do you think?

WHY EACH PSYCHOLOGY SUBFIELD IS AN ECHO CHAMBER?

I should probably say up front that the applied psychology subfields, like forensic psychology, clinical psychology and developmental psychology, are probably the exceptions to this rule, but I want to explore my point first of all. And I want to mention the limits and drawbacks of this question about clinical psychology at the end.

I'll start off by explaining this generally before I explain the flat out weird inspiration that kicked off the idea behind this reflection.

If we take a step outside clinical psychology for a moment and look at the three "main" approaches to behaviour. We have biological, cognitive and social psychology and all of these are fairly divorced from the others and this is great, but bad at the same time.

For example, it is brilliant that biological psychology only looks at our biology and how these processes impact our behaviour. It gives biological psychology researchers the freedom to explore our biology without getting mixed up with cognitive and social psychology.

The same goes for cognitive psychology. It's great that cognitive researchers can investigate our mental health and occasionally tap into biological or neuropsychology without worrying about social psychology variables.

Equally, it is so freeing that social psychologists can focus on how social situations and factors impact our own individual and group behaviour without having messy biological or cognitive factors interfering with the social behaviour.

And yes I know there is some overlap between these three disciplines as seen in social cognition, brain wave activity and how that impacts learning (what I did my dissertation on) and there are a handful of other crossovers too.

Yet my point is still hopefully clear. Each subfield of psychology is fairly or basically exclusively divorced from each other, which has its benefits and drawbacks.

In addition, the entire reason why this reflection is being written in the first place is because of a weird comment a friend of mine said. Now as psychology students we're all used to weird comments, but this comment I found really weird and mind-bending.

"That's cognitive psychology. I don't know if you clinical people are into that,"

Now I completely forget what we were talking

about but I remember we were standing in the computer rooms where we were all testing our participants that day and when she said that I was shocked for a few easy reasons I will show you below (just bear in bear that psychological, cognitive and mental processes are the exact same thing)

Psychotherapy

Clinical **psychol**ogist

Psychological therapy

Cognitive Behavioural Therapy

Those four aspects are absolutely core features of clinical psychology and without those four, our profession could not function but this friend of mine actually believed clinical psychology was NOT interested in mental processes.

Personally, because this friend is great and I really like her, I'm going to be a little kinder than I normally would because this opinion makes no sense to me.

Yes, my friend is a cognitive person by trade and she is obsessed with cognitive psychology but again, she wants to work in clinical psychology. As well as this builds on perfectly from the last reflection, I really want people who want to work in clinical psychology settings to actually understand clinical psychology early on.

Since if she did take any clinical psychology modules or did any sort of clinical research then she would know without a shadow of a doubt that clinical psychology is all about the biological, psychological (cognitive) and social factors that interact together to develop and maintain a mental health condition.

Therefore, the fact that she thought clinical psychology couldn't give a rat's behind about cognitive processes, really hammered home to me just how isolated the theoretical and applied disciplines are.

And this I think is a massive shame because one of the biggest problems in the clinical psychology literature is that it is written by research academics in a way that either isn't understandable or usable by clinical practitioners. Basically making the research next to useless.

This is a problem that might start to be fixed in the future because I know there are clinical psychologists conducting research and lecturing at universities more than ever (apparently), but it is still a problem that needs to be overcome.

Also, if this problem starts with academics and people in the biological, cognitive and social psychology approaches themselves. Then in an ideal world, they would at least be given clinical psychology teaching or something by a real clinical psychologist so they could understand the practical sides of everything.

Since so much of clinical psychology is about practicalities and, at least in the UK, knowing what you can and cannot do in the NHS. This isn't a dig at anyone, it is just my opinions on the whole mess we find ourselves in.

Furthermore, what I really think this is about is

communication and cooperation between the disciplines. I am not saying that the theoretical approach shouldn't do applied research or research that might be able to be adapted into something useful and practical because that is stupid. As well as everyone in academia should have the freedom to research whatever they want if it is legal, useful and ethical.

However, what I am saying is that if we ever want researchers and students and academia as a whole to truly understand the applied disciplines and what clinical psychology actually cares about. There has to be more communication and cooperation across the disciplines and then that would have other benefits as well.

Especially since a clinical psychologist would bring the real-world experience and clinical expertise to a project, and an academic would bring the hard science methodology that clinical psychologists might not have done for years.

There is plenty of room for both if academia allows it to.

The age of echo chambers needs to end and the age of academia afterwards needs to be more useful to applied disciplines, cooperative and have a lot more communication for sure because clinical psychology cares about everything that would help them to decrease the psychological distress of their clients and improve lives.

That is all we care about at the end of the day.

WHY PEOPLE BELIEVE MENTAL HEALTH IS ITS OWN ANGLE IN PSYCHOLOGY?

Sort of continuing with the theme and spirit of the last reflection, in this next one I really, really want to explore why on earth people believe that mental health is its own private angle to understanding human behaviour instead of combining the biological, psychological and social factors in the biopsychosocial model.

Therefore, I'll explain how this reflection actually came to be, then I'll explore why I think this happens before wrapping up with what does this misconception mean for clinical psychology.

How Did This Reflection Come About?

When I was doing my Final Year Project last year, I was working with a wonderful friend of mine and we met because of this project and I worked with her for months as we both did the EEG and behavioural aspects of the project. And the reason why this was a two-person project was because of the timings involved and how complex it got at times, but I do write about this in a book due to come out in 2024.

Anyway, this friend of mine is great, wonderful and amazing. Yet one of the themes of our discussions from time to time was the future and future degrees and careers. She wants to become a clinical neuropsychologist.

And yes, she was one of the three people that inspired the last reflection.

Now you need to realise that in the UK, you have to become a fully qualified doctor of clinical psychology then do two years of work then there's a chance for you to take the extremely specialist clinical neuropsychology degree to become trained as a clinical neuropsychologist.

I know in other countries it is very different.

Anyway, me and my friend were talking one day and the conversation ended up with her saying that she didn't think clinical psychology was interested in biological, psychological or social factors because we were only interested in mental health.

What the fuck?

Now I do honestly understand that she doesn't do clinical modules and I do love her to death (in a friend way only) but I just don't understand why people outside of clinical psychology believe mental health is its own angle.

Why Could This Be?

I already mentioned that these people who tend to believe this are always outside clinical psychology so they don't read clinical psychology books, attend modules or do anything related to clinical psychology, and yet they want to work in the field one day.

That's a topic for another day and I do personally find that headshaking.

Yet I still don't understand this, because what would mental health look like if it's its own angle?

Personally, I have no idea and even more in Volume 3 of this series, I did outline a number of futurist reflections about the future of psychotherapy, psychology and more. Even I don't have the brain power to calculate or hypothesis what mental health would look like without the other three approaches to behaviour.

That's the key here.

It is critical to mental health and it is so engrained in our profession's core that we draw on psychological, biological and social research to fully understand all mental health conditions.

We know as current or future mental health practitioners that biological research alone, cognitive psychology research alone and social psychology research alone is useless. I'll say it, all these things alone and isolated are useless because they only imply that biological factors cause mental health conditions, for example, which is rubbish.

We all know that mental health conditions are a

mixture of interactions between these three types of factors, so whilst alone these approaches are useless to mental health. When clinical psychology starts to combine them then these are immensely useful and they form the foundation of this amazing, great and inspiring profession that we are all apart of.

Of course, I am flat out not saying that it is useless to research all of these separately because that really is the only way to research these things. You need to isolate and control these variables and the more types of variables you try to bring in the hardest your research becomes.

It is just the applying that I am saying is useless if we try to be reductionist.

Overall, when it comes to mental health and clinical psychology being its own separate discipline and angle, that is just beyond silly and it is really headshaking. Biological, social and psychological factors are the lifeblood of the applied subfields and that isn't a bad thing.

What Does This Misconception Mean?

This is a very hard section to write because I am not personally sure. Since I don't believe in this misconception and I am so divorced from the people or group that do believe in this myth that I am only making guesses based on what my friend said.

However, the main problem this misconception causes is that people are avoiding clinical psychology possibly, because they want to research or work in mental health settings using their main approach.

For example, my friend loves cognitive psychology and neuropsychology so she wants to keep researching and working in clinical psychology settings with only cognitive psychology models and theories behind her.

That isn't how the world works, or should work.

For starters she wouldn't be able to get the clinical expertise that she so desperately needs without clinical psychology experience and knowledge, but it is also that the problem with the main approaches is that they are very isolated from the clinical psychology values of topics like lived experiences, the biopsychosocial model, trauma-informed care and so many other topics that make up the core of our clinical practice. Yet these are utterly avoided and completely forgotten in academia research.

Even worse, I have heard plenty of academics from cognitive, social and biological psychology research projects openly or implicitly say that academics know best and there is limited value in service-user data.

That is flat out wrong.

It is our service-users and others with mental health difficulties that are at the heart of modern clinical psychology because these are the people we are trying to help. It is useless if we create interventions for anyone but them, but if academia doesn't see this as important then I am truly concerned the future of research into mental health conditions conducted by non-clinical psychology people.

There is no such thing as the best psychology subfield, but in certain situations I certainly think an argument can be made and this just might be one of those times.

WHY BROADENING OUR DEFINITION OF THERAPY MIGHT BE A GOOD THING?

With each of these reflections I always try to give you food for thought, something interesting or something controversial to really get all of us thinking. But sometimes I just write these reflections so I can express my own thoughts and feelings on the topic and this time, I certainly think this is an interesting and expressive reflection.

Since for a piece of coursework last year, I had to create a poster like the ones that PhD students have to present at conferences on their research. Yet my poster had to be based on a novel type of psychological therapy, so one that had some research but not a lot and wasn't a well-known psychological therapy. It couldn't be Cognitive Behavioural Therapy for example.

Therefore, in my eternal wisdom I decided to

choose "Using dolls for therapeutic purposes: a study on nursing home residents with severe dementia" by Cantarella et al. (2018).

It turned out that whilst I am good at essays and "normal" university assignments I am not as good at posters. Yet during this assignment I was rather interested in the definition of therapy. Since when I found this paper I simply couldn't believe it that these "researchers" were calling playing with dolls "therapy".

I was surprised at that so that's why I choose the topic to do my poster on.

As well as for the sake of clarity, I'll give you some of the bullet points from my poster so you can understand the paper and why this was actually an excellent therapy, and that will set up the rest of this reflection up nicely.

Introduction

- Psychosocial Interventions focus on reducing the behavioural and psychological symptoms of dementia (BPSD).
- Improve well-being and quality of life for dementia sufferers and carers.
- Doll Therapy (DT) consists of giving clients baby-like dolls during therapy sessions.
- Built on attachment theory.
- DT could help people to satisfy their need for closeness and reassurance. Resulting in a reduction of BPSD.
- DT could sustain communication skills, help

people focus on their surrounding environments and prevent social withdraw by providing ready-made topics of conversation.
- Few studies published on DT using good empirical measures.
- Our study examines DT in a nursing home and its efficacy at reducing BPSD and relative distress in carers.

Method

- **Phase 1-** Study protocol discussed with nursing staff and family members. Brief structured interview was done to better understand life before dementia.
- **Phase 2-** SPMSQ given to sample
- **Phase 3-** Lasting 1 week behaviours and attitudes towards dolls or handwarmers were monitored.
- **Phase 4-** 20 sessions of doll or handwarmer use. Objects given to participants 5 times a week for a month. Each session lasted 60 minutes.
- **Phase 5-** Post-test assessments happened 1 week after phase 4.

Discussion And Conclusion

- Only DT group showed significant reduction in BPSD and significant lower levels of distress for carers.
- Suggests DT helps dementia sufferers relieve negative feelings and satisfies attachment

needs
- Our study indicates DT could have several benefits for people with dementia whilst being affordable to services.

And just because I know some of you love limitations. I do understand, limitations can be fun.

Limitations
- Needs larger sample
- Needs a follow study
- Needs to know longer term effects of DT

Overall, the point of the study was to show that by telling people with severe dementia to take part in doll therapy, it would boost their social skills, communication skills and mentally stimulate them. Leading to a reduction in their symptoms and provide cognitive stimulation for them.

That's what the study found.

Therefore, I'll freely admit that I was completely wrong to judge that study first of all and question how mere dolls could be used in a therapeutic setting, because there is good research on it.

Granted, there is nowhere near enough research to make me wholeheartedly believe in the doll therapy, and we do need more research before this is rolled out on a larger scale. Yet the only point I am interested in is how we need to broaden our definition of therapy.

And by this, I mean we all need to be open-minded to how different things, everyday objects and more could be used in a therapeutic way. This is something that all of us are bad at and I know I never will be good at this, but the point is still interesting.

This is even more true, if we think about how the most basic definition of therapy is one or two things (or both). It is a process that leads to a reduction in psychological symptoms, or it is a process that helps people to manage their symptoms better in more adaptive ways.

Yes I know the second definition is a rip-off of Cognitive Behavioural Therapy but this is basically what all psychotherapies aim to do.

Therefore, if we apply those seriously basic definitions to doll therapy then the therapy does lead to a reduction in symptoms.

Due to its used in a structured way.

That's something else I really want to point out because that is a major part of therapy and what separates it from non-therapies. For example, psychotherapies are mainly called talking therapies (even though they are so much more than that) but it is the structure and controlled delivery of CBT that makes it a real therapy.

I guess if the people with severe dementia merely played with the dolls with that slightly structured intervention then the results might have been smaller, or non-existent.

There are a lot of factors that differentiate non-therapies and therapies. Like the research support, its empirical basis, the structure and the expertise needed and more. Yet my point in this reflection is to show that when we really boil it down to almost simplistic levels, there is less than separate professional therapies and new up-coming therapies. Surf therapy, art therapy and dog therapy are only a few examples.

Of course I am not sure that very few of these therapy (especially so-called surf therapy) will ever have the research base of something like Cognitive Behavioural Therapy or Mindfulness-based Cognitive Therapy (if I want to set the bar a lot lower). But if there is research support for a therapy then it is important we don't dismiss it out of hand just because it sounds weird.

I almost did that and that could have been a large mistake.

As a profession we need to open our minds and always be researching, thinking and validating therapies just in case we discover something incredible. CBT wasn't always about, it was developed by a great man and another therapy will be developed by another great man or woman.

And that certainly would be a very exciting idea indeed.

Reference:

Cantarella, A., Borella, E., Faggian, S., Navuzzi, A., & De Beni, R. (2018). Using dolls for therapeutic purposes: A study on nursing home residents with severe dementia. *International journal of geriatric psychiatry*, *33*(7), 915-925.

MEANING OF FICTION, HOPE AND SOME WEIRD LINKS TO CLINICAL PSYCHOLOGY

Whilst I fully admit that I wrote the next two reflections a while ago before I wrote the rest of this book and I'm in a very different headspace now, I still strongly think you need to read these reflections.

Due to whilst they might seem a little unrelated to clinical psychology at first, I do make very stark points in the end that are not only important for our work with clients, but also for ourselves. All future or current clinical psychologists need to take care of themselves too and that is a resounding theme in the next two reflections.

Enjoy.

***

There always comes a point in our lives or week, to be honest, that all of us need to take a step back and actually focus on our own mental health and what we need, instead of what we wish we needed.

I know this will probably end up in the middle of the reflection book I put this in, because unlike all the other reflections in any of these pages, I am writing this one way before I write another reflective book. And even longer before I think about what to include.

Because for once I am being completely and utterly selfish and focusing on my mental health and what I need before others. Of course, and please do not mistake, I am jokingly say that this is selfish because your mental health, your wellbeing and what you need are all some of the most important things in existence.

But if you know me and if you're a podcast listener or a long-term reader, then you might have gotten the sense that I am awful at putting my needs ahead of others.

That's why I'm writing this "reflection" in a book because I have to say to myself that what I need has to help other people to, otherwise it is pointless to "waste" my time journalling for something so trivial.

And I like to think what I want is to reflect on will people everyone to realise the sheer power of journalling, it might help make some people more aware of my lived experiences and it might help others feel less alone in case our difficulties are the same.

At least that is what I tell myself.

What I Want To Reflect On

In Volume 2 of this series, I reflected on an experience of a book that I read and how it affected me positively from a mental health perspective, but now I want to reflect on a book in a similar vein (I cannot confirm what book it is out of concern of being sued for defamation but still) because the book was a gay romance about marriage and it was all rather wonderful until the ending.

Because if you're a romance reader then you know that romances only have one ending, or one ending that is acceptable to readers. The couple, whoever they are, absolutely have to get together and it is what is expected.

And to be fair the story did get that right because the two guys getting married did stay together, but considering the entire point of the book was about gay marriage, how badly the characters wanted it and the word "husband" was in the title. I really expected and so did a number of other people judging by the reviews, you expected the two guys to get married.

Personally, your own beliefs about gay marriage isn't really a focus here in case you were wondering that, but the point of fiction is to make sense and that ending didn't not make sense, and it made me mad.

Because one of the reasons why I occasionally read gay romance is because I am a gay man that did not have the best childhood in gay terms. Due to my family and friendships groups were not gay-friendly so I was trapped in a scary closet hearing lots of abusive language that wasn't aimed at me, but the type of person I was for eight years until lots of things happened, I came out and things are improving. As well as it should be mentioned that there were times that my mental health was horrific and I had so few people to support me.

Anyway, as a person who even now cannot truly see what a future looks like when I am me, able to love who I love and be me, whoever I actually am at this point. Gay romances give me a peek into a world that I could never know for the time being, they give me hope for a brighter future in that aspect of myself and they most importantly allow me to know about dating, relationships and more. An information area that I cannot access at this point in time.

In addition, the first book in this particular series was so amazing because it made me feel like there was actual hope for me, and that I could find love, respect and a relationship. It made me feel amazing, something I don't always feel what it comes to my own sexuality because of other people.

I certainly do not wish to be straight and I do not blame myself for my negativity towards my life in terms of what I can and cannot say or do in terms of being gay. That is just my life at this moment in time, but romances and books are great ways to remind myself that being gay is okay, there are positive feelings of love, caring and boyfriends to experience.

But when an ending messes up this badly, it makes me feel bad because the hope that I, rather unhealthily, place in romance books feels misplace and the messed up ending seriously makes me question my own positions about marriage and love.

Do I think gay marriage is right? Can I see myself ever getting married and being with people? Is there a chance I could ever be with someone I love? Or will I die alone?

Of course I think gay marriage is right, but the others are concerning emotional questions, that I fully admit might sound pathetic to some people. But given the homophobic world I grew up in and the abusive language I was bought up on that was never aimed at me, they are not pathetic but real questions that I hope to answer one day.

But that day is definitely not close by because of the issues of the past I must deal with, that cannot be challenged just yet in case I burn bridges I cannot fix, and currently that is far from a clever idea, and that will not help my survival.

For that is something else about the sheer power of fiction, it really does help you escape everyday life for a little while, so my gay side just normally tries to survive for another day, romance books allow me to escape and allow those unexplored part of me to thrive for the smallest of times in the grand scheme of things, but that is all I need for now.

And I should also note that another thing that slightly irritated me about the book was simply that there was a lot of politicalness in its topics that definitely added depth and made me understand side aspects of the LGBT+ community more than before. But it was almost becoming tedious.

Now I know that fiction is a great vehicle for

some mild politics. You only need to read my mysteries *Theft of Independence*, *Trains, Scots and Private Eyes* and my gay spy romance *Fallen for A Lie* to know my strong support for Scottish Independence despite me being English and really wanting to move to Scotland once it is interdependent. But again those reasons are outside the scope of this reflection, yet if you read those books you wouldn't know I was being overly political.

This book wasn't and again romance books are escapist, not political in nature. A balance must always be maintained, to be honest just like in clinical psychology when it comes to revealing information about ourselves to our clients.

Some information is good and healthy for the therapeutic alliance like I have discussed on the podcast before, but too much is very unhealthy and causes a lot of problems.

One day I will confront my past, move on and try to find out who I actually am when it comes to being gay. But I will admit this romance book that I honestly hate now did teach me one thing about that particular journey when I truly start it, always make sure you're being who you want to be and not what others will want you to be.

It terms of you as a future or current psychologist that might be being a good therapist of certain therapeutic models that you might love, but others disapprove of. But that is okay because it is your career and life so it must be up to you.

So to truly wrap up this reflection (and if you're still reading, thank you and you are amazing), I know I have a lot of difficulties to challenge, confront and deal with from my past at some point. But the day I can do that is far, far away from the day I write this reflection on the 25th August 2022, and I also know I place an unhealthy importance on gay romance books being special to me.

My takeaway message is, there are always things we need to watch for in our past that could haunt us into the future and it is rather remarkable what can end up triggering the pain they cause us, that most days we simply live with.

I was surprised today that awful ending of the romance book triggered the negative feelings with me and that the ending made me feel hopeless, but all that I can unofficially recommend is that we deal with it. I did it tonight by journaling and sharing and trying to make sure my experience could help someone. And finding what helps you is important too.

Just never bottle it up because that never ends well, and believe me when I say I know from personal experience.

I really do know all too well.

A CONTINUATION, POSITIVTY IN TV AND MORE

It turns out I am rather the completist in fact because after the last reflection, I had absolutely no more desire to write reflections based on my own sorting through of mental health, being gay and more, but last night as I write this on 28th August 2022 I decided to watch Netflix's Heartstopper and there are definitely some lessons to reflect on.

And yes, there will definitely be clinical psychology links of different types from tedious to fairly concrete in this reflection.

Overall, if you're wondering what this reflection will contain, it will mainly focused on the lived experiences of gay people, what we face in the negative terms and the hope and escape and love that a sense of community and fiction can provide us with.

As well as it does sort of go without saying but if you haven't watched Heartstopper, then it is brilliant and I cannot recommend it enough. Also I know some people won't find this chapter interesting, but some people might and if these reflections have taught me anything over the past three books, it is that inspiration and a nugget of useful information can hit at the most unsuspected of times.

Therefore, in terms of reflecting and what happened, I basically binged the entire seasons of Heartstopper in a single go. That's easily about 3 and a half hours and I never ever binge TV like that so it was good.

In addition, if you know me personally then you know I do not cry. I am not the sort of person to cry in emotional scenes and to date in my 21 years of living and probably hundreds of thousands hour (I have no idea) of watched TV and movies. I have only ever cried at one thing. One scene in the film Divergent that I watched twice.

And I cried a lot during Heartstopper because there are so many relatable things that the characters say though, and as you'll see there were things that were said as I would have loved someone to say to me.

The Reflections

One of the overall messages of Heartstopper and something that was said repeatedly was *there is nothing wrong with you* (for being gay).

Now this does seem like a well-dub moment because of course if you're gay and if you aren't, you know (or damn well should know) that there is nothing wrong with you for being gay, it's natural and a part of life.

However, even though I have always been comfortable being gay despite my environment that I grew up in. No one has ever said that to me specifically or even remotely in a caring way. I've been completely comfortable being gay since I was 16 or 17, and yet I still would love someone to say to me that there's nothing wrong with me in the slightest.

This is probably down to my environment when I was growing up from all sides. It could have been a longing for someone to care enough to just talk to me and more.

And linking this to clinical psychology a little, our clients do actually come to us for this reason exactly. Sometimes all they want is recognition that they do have a mental health condition and they want solutions, and they want someone on their side.

Due to if you have depression but everyone, including your friends and family, just thinks you're being lazy and sad and silly. Then there is great power in someone telling you that you do have depression, that's okay and as a therapist I am here for your mental health and I'll help you improve your life and decrease your psychological distress.

That's how powerful that small sentence in Heartstopper was for me.

You Don't Ruin People's Lives

Now I'm sure any gay person who has grown up in a homophobic environment, be it at home, school or anything else, can support me here that even if people seriously do not intend it like this. People tend to make comments that make it seem like you ruin their lives by being gay.

You might be ruining their lives because it adds complexities to their relationships with you. You might be ruining them because they wanted grandchildren and apparently you can't give them to them now (even though you can) and so much more.

Or maybe you feel like you're ruining people's lives because you feel like life is more complex now, and it's YOUR fault.

Let me give a heavily cloaked personal example here, so even since I was forced out to two specific family members, whenever girlfriends and more are mentioned by other family members, they always give me a glance like *don't you dare correct them. Just say you're waiting for a girlfriend.*

Equally, these same people don't like me sharing it with other people or other family members, and whatever I mention about hearing homophobia (not that it is ever directed at me because I apparently cannot tell anyone) they always double check that I didn't defend it or whatever.

Personally, I'm like for fuck sake this is ridiculous, I shouldn't have to live like this because I'm fine, I'm not doing anything wrong and I'm not hurting people. Not that I ever actually say it.

But my point is as minority groups, we are sometimes made to feel like we are ruining the lives of others for our existence and that everything is our fault and we are the worse of people for being apparent burdens on others.

Therefore, when I saw a scene on Heartstopper when the main character Charlie was explaining to his sister (if memory serves me) about how he feels like he ruins people's lives. I got that. I got that so badly and when his sister and whoever he was talking to told him he wasn't ruining the lives of others.

I just cried.

Because I honestly could never imagine someone telling me that, I could never imagine a loved one saying it. Or at least in a way that I could believe because they said it in really carefully and meaningful.

And returning to clinical psychology, this is another great job of us current or future psychotherapists, because what we say can and does change lives. We give people hope when there isn't any, we give people a safe space so they don't have to suffer in silence, and most importantly we can sometimes say the things that our clients never realised they needed to hear so badly.

Which is why I love Heartstopper so much because it said some amazing things that I needed to hear so badly, but I just never knew I needed them.

<u>Don't Let People Make You Feel Small</u>

Continuing in the same sort of vein and tapping into the reflection below, but when you've experienced as much abuse and homophobia from many sides as I have, you really do get a bit hopeless, quiet/ suppressed and you feel small.

I never really realised it until one of the Heartstopper characters said something along the lines of *"Don't ever let people make you feel small Charlie,"* and that was something else that really hit me, because they're right.

Why the hell should I have to feel small, pointless and pathetic for doing nothing wrong? Why am I the one in the wrong? And why am I meant to suffer and not the others?

Bullying, abuse and homophobia are all used to make people feel small, but I'm not, you aren't, regardless of your sexuality and I was rather shocked when I heard this, because it sort of felt like something clicked inside me because the character was completely right.

No one should ever be allowed to feel small.

As a result, and tying this to clinical psychology, there are two things to reflect on. Firstly, as future or current psychologists make sure no one ever lets you feel small.

Sure you might be newer, younger or whatever in relation to the idiot being horrible to you, but you are still an amazing person who has been through university, done their clinical training and has a job.

They seriously don't handout clinical psychology jobs for the fun of it. They only give them to amazing people who are the right sort of people and if you have one, you're doing clinical training or you really want to do it. Then you are the right sort of person and don't you dare ever let someone take that away from you.

Because you really are amazing and you should never let someone make you feel small.

You Shouldn't Have To Hear The Hate

Now out of the 8 episodes of Heartstopper, I'll always remember that this is said in the first half of episode 7 because this really did make me cry because as I've mentioned repeatedly over the years I've had so much abuse, homophobia and more from all sides and even though the friends that were perfectly fine with me being gay. I either never told them about the abuse because I was probably concerned they would never fully understand (maybe that was a mistake or not) and if they were aware I don't feel like they really understood it.

Therefore, no one ever said to me to my face that I shouldn't have to deal with the hate, abuse and more.

No one has ever said anything like that to me, so when it was said on Heartstopper. It really did bring up all emotions of like why did I have to deal it with all, why couldn't people apologise for their abuse and why couldn't people just allow me to be me.

And most importantly and personally, why could the most important people in my life be bothered to have a deep conversation with me, so they could understand me, understand the damage they're done and just learn about me like they lied they wanted all those months ago.

I have always said I understand why the two

most important people in my life were hesitant at first, and why it has taken time for them to accept it and everything. But I will not understand why they cannot meet me half way.

I respect them and except not to tell other people, not to publicly proactive and whatever other nonsense I unconsciously promise, but I would like them to meet me halfway and give me the decency to actually understand me.

Instead of turning round to me saying *if you ever wore a dress we would slam our feet down*. And believe me I would NEVER EVER wear a dress, and if they had the decency to talk to me they would know that.

Quickly dipping into clinical psychology here, we are all bound to have clients at some points in time that have experienced hate. Whether this is hate through racism, sexism, homophobia or to be honest one of the other forms of hate in our society, we will have to treat them at some point in our therapy rooms.

And when this happens, it is our job to help them realise the haters are wrong, they are right and that they too never should have had to hear the hate. Because hate is flat out wrong against everyone and that is something that I hope will continue to change overtime.

But whilst we cannot control hate in society, the least we can do as therapists is to make our therapy rooms a hate-free zone, and to be honest you'll probably be a lot more surprised at the sheer benefit that does than you realise.

Overall, as I said subtly (probably not that subtly in the last reflection) I am damaged. I have massive problems with the past, how I was treated and how other people did horrible things to me, and how I was left alone to suffer with so precious few people trying to help me, before they disappeared from my life too.

Those problems will never really go away, at least for the time being but now I absolutely know that I never should have had to endure what I did, and I shouldn't have to hear the hate.

"I Know People Have Hurt You, But I Want You,"

I completely know I'm paraphrasing here but in episode 8 in the last half of it, the Nick Nelson character says to Charlie "I know people have hurt you, but I want you,". Now I don't exactly think it's difficult to imagine what hearing these words meant to someone like me who is frankly as, if not more, damaged as the Charlie Springer character, with bullying from all sides and more. But I will say though thankfully the Charlie character never had homophobia from one side of his life and I am very jealous of him for that.

Anyway, but I was shocked and I cried (yet again) when I heard that because it meant that there was hope.

There was hope for someone with such a tragic and traumatic past as mine could find love, get a boyfriend and actually feel everything a person should feel. Like love, happiness and just someone loves you.

I admit when I typed out the quote in the first paragraph of the section, I shook a little because clearly even now I am still so interested in that idea that just because you're damaged doesn't mean you're unwanted.

And that was a life changing revelation for me.

Linking to clinical psychology before we move on, part of a psychologist's job is actually to provide hope of a better future without mental health difficulties, psychological distress and a negative life. We provide people with so much hope that it is life-changing and before they come into our therapy room they don't see another way.

So I guess in reality this section is just another way to conceptualise what we actually do as psychologists, and why we are so important.

<u>Stop Feeling The Need To Apologize for Everything</u>

Surprisingly enough this section wasn't included at first and I'm adding it in here, because it was a later realisation of mine after I had finished the chapter the first time around. Which surprised me because this is actually one of the clearest points in Heartstopper.

Since to grossly oversimplify, in an effort to make you watch it yourself, is at the begin of the programme it is the Charlie character that is constantly apologising whenever he feels he's done something wrong, and towards the end of the series, it is the Nick character doing the same but Charlie stops it because Nick tells him nothing is his fault.

Then Charlie teaches Nick the same lesson.

Therefore, I really want to reflect on this because it feeds into the sections above, because I understand why the Charlie Character feels like apologising so much and why everything is his fault.

It's because when you have been treated so badly by bullies, haters and the rest for as long as you can remember, you do end up feeling like you not only ruin everyone's lives but everything is your fault. Especially if loved ones did blame you for things for a period of time, as children or young adult we do internalise things.

And this only adds to the sections because as gay people who deal with hate from sometimes everyone for so long, it's hard not to feel like everything in life is your fault, every single thing, every single mistake, every single everything is always your fault.

I know it sounds stupid, but that's what the abuse, the homophobia and the lack of support does to you over time. So I understand, I truly do, the need to apologise for whenever something even slightly goes wrong, because that's also what we're taught in society.

When do you do something wrong you apologise and try not to do it again. As well as this is only amplified when you want to avoid what causes the homophobia or negativity aimed at you.

You just want it to stop.

Therefore, in terms of clinical psychology, I'm sure this connects to co-dependency but I haven't looked into that area too much so I cannot comment on that whatsoever. But what I can comment and reflect on is that sometimes one of our client's maladaptive coping mechanisms will be to be a people's pleaser, someone who overcompensates and just thinks everything they do is flat out wrong.

Because that is what we are taught and even though we know (or I hope we know it) isn't right, it still takes the great steady hand of a psychologist to help us understand why this isn't the case, and how to form better coping mechanisms so we can deal with what the world throws at us.

And that's why psychologists are so amazing.

Therefore, going back to the Heartstopper example, after watching it, I really understand now why we (more me in this case) need to stop apologising, because barely any of the things I do and the things that go wrong are actually my fault.

Most of the time I apologise just as a survival mechanism because if I don't I'm concerned about the chaos that would cause because people just blame me, not because they're targeting me, but because they honestly think it's my fault.

In addition, connecting this to another section above about people loving damaged people (yes I know that's such a bad way to put it) but we need to stop apologising for the damage that others have caused us.

None of us ever asked to be damaged, abused or experience the hate that we do, so why should we apologise for it?

I don't think there really is a reason why we should apologise at all, because it isn't our fault, and the sooner we realise that the better.

I truly believe that.

At the end of the day, stop apologising for the damage that others have done, and make sure you start realising that not everything that goes wrong is your own fault, because it's most likely that it has nothing to do with you.

<u>Be Whoever You Want To Be</u>

Stepping away from the serious stuff for the last few reflection sections, this was definitely one of the major themes of Heartstopper, because you have the Charlie Springer character who is and he is able to be whatever he wants (at least that's my impression). Then you have the Nick Nelson character who I also identify a lot with because the whole point of season 1 is him discovering who he actually is, despite of all his homophobic friends just assuming who he is, and Nick going along with it.

And I loved that major message because I'll explain more in the section below, but I have never really known who I am, or who I wanted to be.

I have no idea what sort of gay I wanted to be, I was forced into a mould of a closeted gay for so many years whilst still being abused that I still have no idea who I am.

Therefore, in the future, when I am more able to in my life because of my current living situation, I will explore myself more and I will decide who I want to be.

Because just like you, our clients and others, we can all be whoever we want. We can be clinical psychologists or not, we can train in Cognitive Behavioural Therapy, Mindfulness Based Therapy or whatever the hell we want.

You deserve to be exactly who you want to be regardless of what anyone else tells you.

Don't Let Your Real Personality Get Buried

This was another little scene in Heartstopper that I did enjoy because Nick didn't want to come out to a girl that asked him out on a date (even though I think the girl guessed and she was amazing towards him in front of his homophobic friends) and he sort of gave a little speech about how confused he felt and that he felt like the real him or his personality had been buried for so long he wanted to see what he actually did want.

Now this really connected with me because my real personality I think is dead. I honestly think whatever gay version of me developed when I first realised I was gay is as dead as a door nail (sorry for the Dickens quote) because I have never known who I am in terms of being gay.

I have no idea if I like the stereotypical gay stuff. I have no idea if I like gay bars. I have no idea what sort of guys I actually like, which for a 21-year-old as I write this I think is pretty sad.

But because of my life I have had to force my gay self into the depths of myself and to use a terrible analogy. All I did in those 8 years before I was forced out to the two most important people in my life, I only looked at guys and thought some were hot, and there was a best friend that I loved for ages and that was a great friendship for me.

But besides from that and when that best friend relationship was destroyed by others' lack of understanding, I have never explored my gay side. Of course not because I never wanted to, but because I was scared of what would happen if I did and if others found out.

So my gay self was left to die for the sake of my survival.

Therefore, could I have been a different person if I was allowed to come out sooner? Maybe. Could I have been less damaged and moved less by Hearstopper if I was allowed to be me? Definitely.

However, I wouldn't change anything about myself because the past is the past, I look towards the future and everything that has happened to me has made me into the person I am today.

The person who podcasts, writes books, has amazing readers and more. That is all because of me and my past, so I would never change it.

But I would like to explore myself in the future, yet even that will only happen in a few years when I can easily (or easi*er*) cut out the people from my life that would abuse me further or change who am I.

Even though they were the ones that forced me to change in the first place.

You Have The Right To Come Out, Not Forced Out

I think this would be a quick section as it's the last one, but the bigger point about this section is that in clinical psychology and life, everyone should have the right to decide who and when they tell them things. It isn't up to anyone else to tell people other things because it is private and it isn't a nice thing to do.

And as psychologists we know that if someone is told to come to psychotherapy when they don't want to, they don't have the capacity or the willingness to change that therapy relies on.

As human beings, we know and can easily think of so many examples of when it is wrong to go behind someone's back and either force them to tell us something, or tell others something that the owner of the secret doesn't want it shared. Due to as we all know it is truly a horrible feeling of betrayal when that happens.

So why is it okay for people to force gay people to tell even that when they know it's dangerous for them to reveal it?

This was something I quickly figured out towards the end of episode 8 of Heartstopper when the Nick character came out to his mum.

Personally, as you know by now, I have not been able or allowed to come out to too many people, but the people I have come out, 3 of them were forced very much against my will, and the only person I truly told out of a genuine want, didn't go well in the end.

For yes, he was fine with people being gay because he was a (there's no polite word for this I'm sorry) shit-stirrer so that never ended well.

Therefore, I suppose all I have any really wanted was to come out to someone on my terms, in my way and just experience coming out to someone positively. Not in a done-and-dusted sort of way that was meaningless like I have done a few times but a real meaningful time.

And to be honest, have someone actually react to it positively.

Like the main reason why I cried at the coming out scene wasn't because of the coming out itself, but because even though the mother (played by the amazing Olivia Coleman) was calm and smiling, she actually said "I'm over the moon for you,"

Now don't get me wrong, I have never believed in big announcements or over-the-top rubbish about being gay, but just to have that sort of positive reaction would just be stunning, instead of cowered, embarrassed secrecy.

Deserving:

To wrap up this long chapter that I've personally loved, and I really never intended it to be this long but it turns out there was a lot to unpack for both myself and clinical psychology. I want to wrap up this chapter with a message of hope for me, psychologists and any gays that might be reading this.

As psychologists, I have written before about the utter crap psychology faces from the idiots that don't believe psychology is a science or anything that is worth the time of day. But as long as you work hard, do the clinical training and always try to be the best you possibly can, then you deserve anything.

You deserve to become a clinical psychologist, you deserve to be working in a clinical psychology job and you most importantly deserve to be happy.

And as I mentioned earlier, don't you dare let people to make you feel small and weak and like you don't belong there, because you do.

You are truly amazing. Not everyone can go through university, do the clinical training and then get a job in clinical psychology, so you really are special for being able to get there.

Just never forget that.

Finally, for the gay people reading (if there are any), the really big mean for me about Heartstopper and the thing that actually made me just sit, think and relax for an hour after finishing my binge, was that it truly shows us how gay people do deserve everything that straight people have.

We deserve to have boyfriends, love and relationships. We deserve to have amazing people around us that make us feel great, we deserve friends and family that love us and we deserve never to have to hear the hate.

And even though I am ending this reflection and I am seriously waiting for season 2 and 3 of Heartstopper on Netflix over the coming years (which I will so watch alone probably because I don't want to embarrass myself crying), what I have reflected on today will not end.

These lessons, insights and realisations will live on, because they are true and they are amazing things that all of us gay people deserve to remember and realise that we are never the problem, we don't ruin lives and we deserve love.

The most important thing of all.

WHY DO YOU NEED TO MAKE SURE YOU ENJOY YOUR CLINICAL PSYCHOLOGY JOURNEY?

As you could probably tell from the middle of the book about how I linked my own mental health and the Netflix series Heartstopper to clinical psychology, some of these reflections aren't written with the rest, and the next two are no different.

Since I'm writing this one in early April 2023 because I have basically finished my university undergraduate degree with only three exams to go in May 2023 and then I'm done as an undergraduate completely. Then I'll go on to do a Masters in October and continue my clinical psychology journey.

Yet I want to reflect on this because this is an end, this is an end of a 4 year journey (because I did a Placement year or a Year In Industry as it's sometimes called) and I want to do a mini-reflection on my time in regards to clinical psychology, before making some inspirational point about clinical psychology later on.

However, if you're on my psychology email list (which you really should be because you get a ton of great information, behind the scenes action and discounts) then last night as I write this, I sent out an email starting with the following two paragraphs:

"As I enter the last week of lectures and my time at university comes to a close before our exam season that will be done online from the comfort of my own home, I definitely have mixed feelings because even though I'll be returning to Kent in October for my Masters. This is the end of a massive four-year journey and I think there will definitely be aspects of it that I miss, like my friends and the lecturers that I've been working closely with in this past year. Yet I am also looking forward to postgraduate and moving onto the next milestone in my life.

Yesterday this really did hit home to me because I was going up to campus from the car park (a good ten minute walk), there was no one about, it was a beautiful sunny day and it just struck me that after Thursday I won't be doing that basic walk again as an undergraduate. It's weird but things are certainly changing,"

I want to reflect on this because that last line is extremely true. Whenever we end a degree, a stage of our lives or something that is extremely important to us then this does feel weird and it feels like we're treading on uncertain times.

Now I will freely admit that I am mildly autistic so change is always relatively challenging for me and I am so, so much better with it now than I was younger.

However, for the past four years I have been working towards this moment, getting my masters and then working towards becoming a clinical psychologist. And now that the first major step is done, I am relieved but also surprised.

I am so relieved because I am now done with my undergraduate. I will have my degree in a few months and I will be the second member of my family to get a degree (but the first to a science and "real" degree) and that is a massive achievement and I am so happy about it.

Also, I am extremely happy that I have managed to get a degree and how far I've come as a person who struggled to write academically in my first and second years. As well as my confidence has vastly improved as a result of my degree and my Outreach work for the university.

I am willing to say that I am an entirely different person to who I was back in 2019 when I started my degree. Also, I did come out to my parents which whilst is a lot of different discussion, it means that I still live with the homophobia and trauma of my younger years but I am no longer scared for a range of reasons which I might talk about one day in case it helps others but not now.

I am a completely different person and that is a great thing.

However, I still have a few petty mixed feelings because this is an end of a great thing for me. I have loved my undergraduate degree, even in my first and second years when I was struggling I still loved it. I loved my learning and developing my knowledge even further.

My Final year has had to be my best because of

the great project supervisors, my friends and other people that I've met along the way.

Nonetheless, this is still a nervous time for me because with the end of my undergraduate, yes it means change which I am always slightly uncomfortable about. Yet this also means leaving people as we all go our separate ways and whilst I will always keep in contact with these great people. It means I will have to begin again the search for new friends, new connections and new everything.

And whilst that is simply life in all honesty and I know I will be fine, it is the uncertainty that I am always unsure about.

This is my point and how this links to clinical psychology. We are all on a journey towards something in psychology, and if you're reading this book then I think you're looking for something at clinical psychology. Whether you're a first year psychology student, a Masters or DClinPsych student, we are all on different legs of our psychology journey.

We will always have to change, adapt and learn. That is what I love about the clinical psychology journey and I love how it will always challenge me.

And yet that is the real point of this reflection, if we always focus on the endpoint, the ultimate destination then we do miss out, we miss out on making the journey worthwhile and interesting and that would be a mistake.

Your degree (whatever one you're doing) is something worth investing in not only for the endpoint and academically, but socially and experimentally too. I now know that there were tons of research and other paid opportunities within the School of Psychology in my first and second years that I so badly wish that I had taken advantage of.

Equally though, I understand why I didn't. I was not a confident person or a person who could believe they could thrive academically and the lecturers and academic staff at the university, I saw them as cold and distant and I wasn't one of their favourites. Thankfully, my placement year changed all that and it was the best decision I ever made.

Overall, my point is, do not just focus on the end goal of your clinical psychology journey. Please make sure that you stop, focus and enjoy all the opportunities that each stage of your degree offers because I can promise you if you miss them, then you will regret it.

Of course never get weighed down with regrets but definitely take every single opportunity you can, because it's a hell of a lot of fun and it certainly makes the journey richer, more fascinating and certainly more interesting.

THE MOST IMPORTANT QUESTION IN RESEARCH

If you were expecting this to be a light-hearted and a very free of controversy reflection then I hate to say that I'm going to disappoint you but I think that this could be one of my most important reflections ever written, because this is a very important topic close to my heart because of a friend I made recently.

Who will I harm with my research?

That I strongly believe is the most important question to ask yourself when you conduct research in existence, and I'll explain the situation and then I'll make this more general with clear links to clinical psychology.

Recently I made a transgender friend who was a biological female and is now a man, he's great, wonderful and he is brilliant. We met properly at an Outreach event where we paired up and in-between the work we were actually doing, we were talking about journeys, all the hate we experienced and it was nice to talk to someone we had had a negative experience surrounding family like I did.

Yet the sources of our hate were different, because whenever people hate something they always get to justify it. For me, religion was used to justify the hate for me and who I was. For him, it was academic research and that was what dawned this reflection.

Later on he sent me the research article that his parents used to say he was mentally wrong and fucked up, I read it, I understood his annoyance at it because it was bad research.

Now I would honestly give you the link to it but it was bad research, it isn't ethical research and it focuses on hate.

Since the current, mainstream dialogue around being transgender, very similar to being gay, is that it isn't a choice and it is a part of you that you are aware of a long time and you typically notice that you are different from straight people from a relatively early age.

I knew I wasn't straight when I was around 13 years old, and my transgender friend realised this about the same time. Note, I didn't say we had personally excepted this part of ourselves, only that we realised we were different. I mention that just in case you know of people that say that realised they were LGBT+ later on in life. That's perfectly validate too.

However, the research in question wanted to question this and propose an alternative idea called Rapid Onset Gender Dysphoria (ROGD).

There are two important things to note here.

Firstly, RODG is not endorsed, believed in or acknowledged by any official body in psychology, government or anything. This is simply a damaging theory that some "researchers" are trying to put forward to explain why being transgender develops and this theory doesn't really tap into psychological or social factors. As well as because this theory is very out-there and goes against the larger mainstream narrative that trans people (the people that actually go through this process) support, this theory isn't evidence support or even fleshed out.

This theory believes that gender dysphoria (the mental health condition of is where a person doesn't identify or believe they match their biological sex or gender) just suddenly develops and this isn't something a trans person develops over a number of years.

Secondly, I seriously NEED to stress here that I have absolutely no problem whatsoever with people researching alternative theories. I know as a person who loves clinical psychology how critical this is, because if no one else research alternatives to the serotonin or other biological interventions to depression. Then Cognitive Behavioural Therapy and a ton of other psychological therapies never ever would have been created.

Alternative theories are flat out critical to clinical psychology, the wider literature and wider society.

However, we have to acknowledge that trans people are still a group of human beings that are struggling and fighting to be legally recognised and they are under extreme amounts of scrutiny at the moment to get access to basic human rights.

Therefore, the current mainstream theory and narratives that realising you are trans is a deeply personal journey that you know deep in your core what your true gender identity is with this journey taking a very long time to discover and this isn't a choice. This supports that trans people should be recognised both socially and legally.

That supports trans people as equal to the rest of us.

Yet for a theory to come into the world and question this, and propose that trans people suddenly develop this identity overnight with no thought at all and this is some strange phenomenon that needs to be extensively questioned. This isn't helpful and this is extremely damaging.

Some evidence for how damaging this theory is comes from the original bad research that went to an online forum of parents writing about how they dealt with their child being trans.

There is nothing wrong with this group of people in the slightest, I can truly understand that from their own perspective that this was a scary and sudden change in their child's behaviour.

My problem with this being "research" is that the data sample was only from transphobic people and people that were ashamed, embarrassed and outraged that their children were trans. The researcher didn't go to supportive parents or even trans people themselves for extra data.

Why?

Maybe this was because the researchers only wanted one type of data or one side of the academic argument, and this is my problem with this research.

This theory, this idea, this researcher has proposed a theory that actively harms a group of people that want legal recognition for who they are and this only increases the struggles they face. As well as it is even worse that the research the theory is based on isn't evidence base, it doesn't take into account what supportive parents say nor does it take into account the very opinions or facts from the very trans people this theory discusses.

Modern research would never write about depressed people or autistic people before researching the target population itself, so why is it okay to do the same for trans people?

I know the vast, vast majority of modern clinical psychology would agree with me, but it still shows that whilst we always need to be researching, expanding our knowledge and wanting to improve the literature, we must always think about the possible impact our research has on a vulnerable group of people.

I know not everyone will agree with me, and that's okay to the extent that I know this is a challenging topic. But the truth is that as future or current clinical psychologists, the research we do will always have an impact on innocent people.

Whilst I know 99.9% of research already does this brilliantly, it is imperative that the research we do only helps innocent people and cannot be twisted in a way that harms them.

HOW ANGER DRIVES ACTION?

When I was reading the May 2022 issue of The Psychologist by the British Psychological Society, I read a very interesting piece about how anger drives us, as humans, towards some kind of action and that is certainly an idea that I think we need to reflect on.

Not only from the clinical psychology viewpoint, but also because of how we as current or future psychotherapists and general people are affected by anger driving us towards action.

For example, if we start off generally before narrowing in on clinical psychology, the world is filled with anger and injustice at times, and at least that is what the news definitely makes us feel at times. And whilst the news is designed to get a rise out of us and make us angry, it isn't always a bad thing that anger turns into action.

It is bad if we watch something on the news for example and that drives us to violently protest, smash up shops and burn down buildings. That is wrong, but equally I do understand that certain things do provoke enough strong emotion to drive people to do that sort of thing. As well as like always the debate about right and wrong is subjective and very much beyond the scope of this book.

Yet if we look towards anger bringing about positive change and action then this has always been the case throughout history, or at least modern history. For instance, if black people and LGBT+ people didn't get annoyed, feed-up and outraged by their constant mistreatment, murder and being treated differently from other law-abiding citizens. Then this never would have led to the stonewall riots, what Rosa Parks did and the events that followed and everything that allows civil rights and equality to function today. That was in the 60s and onwards.

Then if we go back even further towards the start of the 20th century with the suffragettes and the suffragists (the difference is very interesting so I do recommend researching it for yourself), then if women didn't get angry about their mistreatment and how they were barred from doing almost everything in society. Then women would never be allowed to vote, be more than mothers and be more than a mere sex object for men.

Of course I am flat out not saying that modern society is perfect because it seriously not, but these are just some historical examples about how anger leads to positive action and change. Granted some the suffragettes did have questionable methods at times.

Then this is still something we can see in society today from the peaceful climate change protests, to the protests surrounding Scottish Independence and the protests surrounding Black Lives Matter and more. All of these are peaceful for the vast, vast majority of the time and this all came from anger about a situation and people wanting to change it to improve their lives.

Overall, anger is a powerful force for good if used correctly and anger can definitely bring around a lot of good action that improves society. Of course at the time, these protests and these people are seen as crazy, weird and far-left nutters, but history thankfully remembers the suffragettes and others as heroes.

I only hope the modern examples I gave are given the same honour in the history books.

Anyway, if we narrow on in our own profession and apply this idea to clinical psychology then I have to admit that the results are even more stark and easy to see when you realise what we're looking at.

The easiest example of Cognitive Behavioural Therapy, that basically came from anger about the current ideas about how to treat people. At the time it was pretty much all about drugs, drugs and more drugs but there was a clear need for something else. Aaron Beck and basically every single psychotherapist since has been working towards divorcing mental health from the medical model and emphasising a biopsychosocial approach.

Personally, looking back, I write these reflection

books because I am angry to various extents about various things. For example, depending on where I place this reflection in the book you might have read my Psychology At Pride Events and The Most Important Question In Research reflections.

Both of those reflections came from my anger about psychology's awful past with the LGBT+ community and I was (and I still am) disgusted at the research or motivation behind Rapid Onset Gender Dysphoria and how that pointless theory negatively impacts so many lives.

Then if we look at my books and podcast episodes, there are certainly chapters, sections and episodes that I do out of anger because I want to help raise awareness and dispel so many harmful deadly myths.

Hell, I wrote an entire book about suicide because I was so angry with how society treats these people that so desperately needs help. And if you check out my Applied Psychology book, I write the entire section on online hate and Incel ideology because I find it so disgusting that people want to legalise rape and beating women.

It is disgusting so I turned it into action by helping to raise awareness.

Furthermore, if we look at clinical psychology some more, our profession is far from perfect. If we look at the UK, our mental health services are on their knees, there is never enough funding or staff and the waiting lists are beyond stupid. That is what I'm angry about and a ton of clinical psychologists are too so that is why we all want a better NHS that is more fit for purpose.

Some people turn this anger into action by working in the NHS to make sure there is at least one more staff member that can hopefully improve lives. Other people look at the mess of the NHS and go private (which I have to admit isn't that helpful) and other people campaign, write to their MPs and just do something else to protect the NHS and our mental health services.

There is a lot we can do but the real purpose of this reflection is to help you to realise that anger is only bad if you use it destructively.

Anger can be a great, amazing, powerful force for good if we allow it to be. So if you take anything from this reflection then maybe, you should allow yourself to tap into anger more and see what productive healthy action it can inspire you to bring.

As long as you help to make the world a better, more equal and more desirable place to live then anger seriously isn't an enemy. It can be a great friend in a dark moment.

ANOTHER EXAMPLE OF THE POWER OF LANGUAGE (A GREAT ONE FOR PARENTS)

If you've been a long time reader of the series then you know that I do enjoy talking about language, terminology and more every once in a while, so keeping in with that theme I want to talk about it in this reflection book.

Now just in case you haven't read me before, I want to stress the basics first of all. For example, many in modern clinical psychology don't like to use terms like disorder, patient, disease and problems.

Since because all of these terms come from the medical model approach and they're very blaming language and they aren't helpful.

For example, a person doesn't have a mental health problem, they have a difficulty. Since a problem sounds like it is their fault, their problem, so they need to stop wasting the time of mental health services and solve their problem. Whereas you don't get those negative connotations with mental health difficulty.

Secondly, a person doesn't have a mental health disorder or disease because they make it sound like a person has a physical condition that can simply be cured with some drugs and then they will be magically "fixed". Mental health doesn't work like that because mental health conditions are part of who a person is so you cannot cure or fix them.

Instead the entire aim of modern clinical psychology is to decrease their psychological distress, improve their lives and this is typically done by teaching the client more adaptive coping mechanisms. This is even more important when we realise that we, as people and mental health employees, only ever see the coping mechanisms.

Such as we never see depression itself, it doesn't pop out of a person's head and say hello, does it? We only see them never wanting to socialise, them wanting to stay in bed forever and them having a depressed mood. As well as then in therapy and therapeutic conversations we see their negative automatic thoughts in conversation, their attention biases and all the other symptoms of depression.

We never see depression itself. Only the results.

Also, just for the sake of clarity, I am flat out NOT saying mental health conditions don't exist, I am simply saying what we see.

Therefore, instead we use the mental health condition, not disorder or disease.

Finally, for this introductory stuff, we don't use the term patient because again, it is a very medical model term. We have mental health patients because they aren't diseased, curable or anything else. We have mental health clients that we can help, treat and improve their lives.

The New Example I Want To Explore

The inspiration for this reflection came from the May 2022 issue of The Psychologist and the main focus of the issue was on comfort food. And whilst I didn't particularly care about the topic because the psychology of comfort food, well, I just don't find that comforting.

However, at the back of the article, there was an interesting section that is great for parents, and if you are a parent certainly keep reading. The section was talking about how a parent's use of language around food can make kids less fussy about food.

That's right parents. There is a psychological trick to make children less fussy.

The problem with the question is "Do you like your dinner?" is that the idea of liking something is very fixed and it doesn't change much once the opinion is formed. Therefore, if a kid doesn't like the feeling of chicken or something then they will be very fussy about chicken because they don't like it.

However, if you reframe the question to something like "Are you enjoying your food?" then you are asking them an entirely better and different question to the first. Since the idea of enjoyment can change, isn't fixed and it certainly changes over time, even over the time of dinner.

For example, last night as I write this, I had a chicken kebab with my family and I was really enjoying the chicken when I started it. It was juicy, succulent, very well seasoned, it was brilliant. I was seriously enjoying it. Although, I do regret having a large because towards the end of it, I wasn't enjoying it so much, and it wasn't as amazing as before.

Therefore, you can see in that personal example that enjoyment can change rather quickly and it can change from mouthful to mouthful. Meaning what you're effectively saying to your kid with that question is the following:

"Are you enjoying your dinner at that moment in time? If not, keep eating you might enjoy it in a moment,"

Bang.

If you're a parent that I definitely recommend that idea and that is something I'm going to try and educate my family on in the next few months because we are expecting a new baby in the family. So whilst nothing in these books are ever official advice, you might want to look at this technique.

How Does This Link To Clinical Psychology?

I'm aware that this fits into clinical psychology in two main ways. The first one is a bit tenuous but it is still important. We all know as uncles, aunts, whatever that having kids is stressful and delightful, and it is a nightmare when kids do not want to eat a particular food because they aren't enjoying it.

It is so annoying and yes, I think everyone jokes or thinks or dreams about force-feeding their kids at times. I know you do deep down.

Therefore, I really do hope that this little tip will help parents and the extended family to decrease the amount of stress they have about mealtimes, and then this has added psychological benefits to. Since as a parent you do worry about a lot of things about your child so the fact that we can decrease one single thing can actually have a massively positive impact.

Secondly, this is another great example of the power of language. Now I do already know this because of my fiction writing, but in a clinical context, this only highlights how important your language, your words, your tone of voice is in psychotherapy.

Overall, be mindful of language, think about the current language we use in clinical psychology I know Borderline Personality Disorder is effectively banned now because it is so, so inaccurate and it is now replaced with Complex Emotional Needs.

Language will always be evolving and that is a great thing, but clinical psychology needs to keep up because our language does inform public opinion, public perception and our client's perceptions of themselves.

Just a few important things to consider.

WHY PSYCHOMETRIC AND PERSONAL GOALS ARE CRITICAL IN PSYCHOTHERAPY?

Continuing with a very minor theme of this book, this was a brilliant nugget of information that a lecturer mentioned last year during a lecture, where she mentioned that with her clients she always likes to use psychometric tests and goal or person-oriented goals (a better way to put it to be honest) and in this reflection to help reflect on why she is absolutely right.

Firstly, we absolutely have to use psychometric tests in psychotherapy for a few reasons, as well as each of them are critical in their own right. For example, psychometric tests, like your depression, anxiety or autism questionnaires are so important to understand how severe a client's mental health condition is. Then we can use this information to adapt our approach and help them better.

Another reason why psychometric measures are

important is because the NHS, in the UK at least, loves them and since clinical psychology is a science, we always need to gather empirical data. Psychometric measures is one such method of collecting data.

Therefore, psychometric measures help to keep the bosses and our employers happy which is always nice, it means we can continue to empirically show that psychotherapy works and clinical psychology is a science.

All of those are critical to our profession.

However, as we know, psychotherapy is a relationship between the therapist and the client. Let me put a simple question to you, do you think our clients give a rat-ass's about our psychometric measures?

Probably not.

Our clients don't understand them, they probably don't understand how important they are in providing us with the information we need for the therapy, they certainly don't know how the NHS works in regards to empirical data and they definitely will not see the point in them.

That's okay.

Especially, because they are coming to us with a mental health condition that gives them clinically significant levels of distress, impaired functioning and they want us to help them. Therefore, when we turn round and effectively say, *of course I'll help you but I want you to do two or three questionnaires first*. They probably aren't too happy.

That's a generalisation but I think my point is still clear.

Furthermore, after they've done the initial questionnaires or any over psychometric tests they need to do, if a therapist says to them, *by the end of the therapy we'll reduce your depression score by ten*. I know that is a random figure but the client will still just nod and they won't understand what that means for them.

That is an issue because if they don't understand what they're going to get out of it from the start, then why would they want to remain engaged throughout and during the hard times?

They might not.

As a result, this is why personal goals and asking a client what do they want to get out of the therapy is a very good idea. Since not only will that help the client realise what they want, it could have the added benefit of the client trusting and liking the therapist more, as the client will realise that the therapist values their input.

That's even more important for the clinical interview and the formulation.

A client with depression might say that they want to be able to wake up in the morning without feeling like their life is rubbish and they might as well stay in bed all day. That could be the goal that means everything to them and that's valuable information.

Again, not only does that tell us, as current or future therapists, that the client struggles with getting out of bed but it means that they value this, and this value can be a good reminder of why they are in therapy when it gets tough. Therapy always gets tough in the end.

Equally, a client with social anxiety might just say that they want to be able to go into a lecture theatre without feeling like the walls are closing in on them and everyone is staring at them and the ground is going to swallow them alive.

Another benefit of this type of information and this personal goal is that it gives a therapist an ideal of the direction to take the therapy in. That direction might not be something the therapist thinks is a place they need to go immediately because there is therapeutic work to do before they could ever hope to tackle that lecture theatre fear, but it is something for later.

And I know I occasionally hammer on this point, but when it comes to therapy, we are asking a vulnerable, scared person that is experiencing hell to open up to us as a complete and utter stranger, their deepest, darkest fears. We cannot just expect them to instantly do that without trusting us.

And if a simple little question, like what do *you* want out of this therapy, is a way to start that dialogue or at least make it more likely to happen. Then that is a very powerful thing and a very good idea to start using it.

I know that the first one or two therapy sessions are a little hard to get someone to open up too, but even this question might remind them in those sessions or the later sessions, that you, the therapist, are on their side, they can trust you and you will support them no matter what (within limits of course).

And I also think that personal goals are a lot more interesting for therapists too. We all love science, we love the scientific method but it is so dry at times. Sometimes the hard science stuff can be boring as well, but if we have something as interesting and powerful and motivating as a personal goal to help someone towards so we can see the light in their eyes when they finally achieve it. Then that is immensely powerful.

Not for our clients, but for us too and that will definitely make helping the brave, courageous client who has the will to walk through our doors even more rewarding.

And that is why clinical psychology is a great profession.

THE VALUE OF INFORMALLY TALKING TO SERVICE USERS

I was reading the June 2022 issue of The Psychologist by the British Psychological Society (only a year overdue) and there is a great interview with an author of a new (well, new then) forensic psychology book and there was a single little line that caught my eye and I wholeheartedly believe that line.

The best thing anyone can do if they want to go into clinical psychology, forensic psychology or any applied psychology field is to informally talk with service users.

I know this isn't a business psychology book and I have to admit that I think it would be hard for these people to talk with their clients. I suppose a person interested in business psychology would have to talk to business owners which might not be easy.

But still.

The reason why talking to service users is beyond valuable, I might even say it is worth more than gold and diamonds, is because these are the people who we are trying to help, these are the people that know what they are experiencing and these people know exactly what is and isn't working for them.

For example, it was because of a great campaign done by service users that the term Borderline Personality Disorder was dropped and replaced with Complex Emotional Needs, because Borderline Personality Disorder is a useless term. It doesn't explain what the clinical population goes through at all.

It is because of service users that mental health services have improved so much over the years, coming up with new ways of working, new ways of functioning and creating new initiatives.

The one clinical psychology phrase I always remember is *the psychologist is the expert in the therapy, the client is the expert in themselves.* And that is why as current or future psychologists, we absolutely have to listen and talk to service users, because they are the experts in living with mental health conditions.

That is invaluable knowledge to listen to.

Additionally, if we move onto the point about talking to them informally then the reason why this is important because as we know as human beings ourselves, whenever we talk formally about something we are very guarded, protective and we don't open up easily. We don't tell people our secrets, the worse things about ourselves and we certainly don't talk about anything that could cast us in a bad light.

I think we can all agree on that from our own experiences of just living in the world.

However, I know from personal experiences that if you talk to someone informally, not in a professional sense then they are a lot more likely to open up. As well as whilst you cannot do this for safeguarding reasons, it is like when it is just you and someone else alone in a room alone with no other ears about, you are a lot more likely to get juicy information from those other people. That's worked tons of times for me in the past when I've wanted to get extra information from lecturers, teachers and Outreach members of staff and many more people.

That just goes to show how important it is to talk to someone informally and "off the record" so to speak. You're a lot more likely to get the "truth" and the juicy and valuable pieces of information that you wouldn't get otherwise.

How would you get to talking to people informally?

Honestly, this will be hard and this why as much as I would never want this change, at the time I was disappointed that I didn't get a hospital or more clinically focused placement during my year in industry. Since I wanted to get the chance to talk to real clients, learn about them and their lives and help them.

The only real way to informally talk to service users is to get a job or volunteer at a mental health service or a charity that works with people with mental health conditions. This way you can interact with them, build up a rapport with them and maybe if they want to you can talk with them informally. There is nothing wrong with that as long as you follow your workplace's rules and guidelines and you don't break safeguarding rules.

This is why I am very keen on getting a part-time or volunteering position very soon, and hopefully by the time this book's published, I will have a position at a mental health service so I can start learning from service users.

However, if you aren't in a position to do the above suggestion, because you might still be early on in your degree or something similar, then you might want to do one of the following options we'll talk about.

You can read a ton of books on the topic, because there is a lot of books written by people with mental health conditions about their experience. I know I've seen books written by suicidal people, depressed people and I know autism is an amazing area of nonfiction. These are all good tools because authors can be very personal in the writing, I think I'm living proof of that.

Another method is to watch videos on YouTube or another platform about people talking or being interviewed about their experiences. It is the same idea and you definitely hear some great and really bad experiences. Both are extremely educational.

Finally, something I do rather like about psychology and clinical psychology in particular is that it attracts people with mental health conditions, trauma and other features that the general population doesn't have. Of course I'm not saying that every single person who does clinical psychology has a mental health condition, they seriously don't, but some people will.

I always remember my final year clinical psychology modules had a woman with Complex Emotional Needs in the group, two people had experiences of trauma and another person had bad anxiety.

Therefore, if you did want to talk to people in your degree then maybe just look out for people in your modules and just ask them. Of course, you have to be extremely respectful, polite and you need to be friends with them first because you don't know how they feel about talking about their condition with strangers and in public. Especially to another psychology student who's basically only asking because you want to learn about their condition.

But it is another option, yet just be respectful and friendly. Do not *use* them to learn at all.

Overall, service users are some of the most important teachers in clinical psychology. They are the people that make our job possible, they are the people that are living through the conditions and they are the people that we want to help, so their input is honestly worth more than gold to our profession.

So if you can, definitely listen to them, value them and get to know their story. It might be more fascinating than you ever thought possible.

WHY PSYCHOLOGY ORGANISATIONS AT PRIDE EVENTS IS INTERESTING?

If you're a long time reader of this series then you know that I always, always try to include at least one LGBT+ reflection in each book because it is interesting and they are always thought-provoking. Also, if you read [Volume 3](#) of the series, you might be aware that I am always behind on issues of The Psychologist.

Therefore, what happens is when I eventually get around to reading the magazine by the British Psychological Society, I make notes of interesting things that I want to reflect on and in the June 2022 issue, I saw a small section of how the BPS was attending London Pride in June 2022 as part of a group of organisations in the parade.

Now this is something that is fascinating to me because I questioned why the organisation would want to march in the parade, and I have never been to a Pride event so I don't actually know what they're like, but it is interesting because of psychology's past.

Of course, the BPS wants to show their unwavering support for the LGBT+ community in the face of increasing adversity from policymakers all over the world. So this is something that I am truly grateful for, but when it comes to LGBT+ and psychology, this is something that hasn't always seen eye to eye.

In preparation for this blog post I checked out the history of the BPS, psychology and the LGBT+ community. I found a few interesting things.

We all know that it was psychology that decided to label homosexuality as a mental "disorder" up until the late 70s. I know this was in line with societal beliefs at the time and far before the 1970s, but considering that in the UK, homosexuality was decriminalised in 1967. Psychology could have been a game changer and also decided to change its thinking about it being a mental health condition.

Then again, I suppose looking back at the world they lived in, they sadly would have argued that having depression isn't illegal and that's a mental disorder so why shouldn't homosexuality?

Looking back this is flat out and even at the time I think this was extremely wrong, but still psychology labelled homosexuality as a mental disorder and wanted people to get "treated" by getting tortured.

That is exactly what conversion therapy is and that is why it should be banned completely, and I truly welcome and thank all the countries that have banned it outright.

Anyway, psychology allowed people to go willing and unwillingly through torture to "correct" something that didn't need fixing. And if we apply this to modern clinical psychology, even today, we never ever seek to cure or fix a mental health condition, we only seek to help people create more adaptive coping mechanisms for their mental health difficulties and conditions to decrease their psychological distress, as well as improve their lives.

Psychology led to tons of people getting tortured for no reason, and I think we can agree that even by the standards of the time, electrocuting people for being gay was extreme.

Another thing that was interesting about my initial research (and all of this is on the BPS website in case you want to check it. All I typed into Bing was something about the BPS and homosexuality and the article popped up), is how psychology journals published research.

The BPS article mentioned that up until the 1980s, the publication of the research showed that homosexuality research was always focused on homosexuality as a medical and mental disorder that needed to be assessed, treated and erased.

Then in the 1980s, homosexuality research dropped massively because it wasn't seen as a mental disorder anymore (thank God) and then this research was only really published in the British Journal of Social Psychology because the research focused on how homophobia and discrimination against LGBT+ (or back then Gay and Lesbian people) where societal issues.

Therefore, it's interesting to see how clinical psychology has changed its perception over time thankfully and how psychology has continued the tradition of seeing homosexuality as a mental disorder long after it was decriminalised.

Now the reason why I mention this is because when something becomes decriminalised, it is meant to help make people's perceptions of whatever it is as more positive.

Psychology could have helped with that.

Psychology could have got rid of the mental disorder label and it could have focused earlier on anti-homophobia and discrimination research. This could have been encouraged and done at the American Psychological Association level because they created the DSM and it could have been done at a journal-level. Since journal editors could have been harsher and more critical of this so-called research looking at homosexuality as a mental disorder.

But it didn't.

Of course I know full well that I am writing as a gay man in 2023 who has experienced a lot of homophobia, hate and negative mental health because of it, so I am sure some of what I am saying is a little biased.

But I am trying to look at both sides.

Whatever way you cut it psychology has a

negative past when it comes to the LGBT+ community, and this is why psychology organisations going to Pride events, showing their support and showing that the profession changed is something I am very happy about.

Since as I've written before about the dire lack of diversity within clinical psychology and why this negatively impacts our clients, but if people actually see psychology supporting this minority and other minority groups over time. Then this is something, a single small action, that could make someone realise that maybe, just maybe psychology is a profession for them.

Then that person could go on to become a clinical psychologist, help people and improve lives.

We do live in interesting times and I hope that organisations do continue to show that psychology is for everyone no matter who you are, because we desperately need everyone in psychology no matter their class, race, gender or sexuality. We need everyone.

Everyone can bring something different to our work and profession and we never know when a client will walk through that door and need something we cannot offer them because of who we are, but if diversity increases in clinical psychology. Then there's a good chance we can easily find a therapist for them that matches their background.

That is the positive, empowering and amazing future of our profession if we allow it to be, and thankfully at the moment it looks like we are certainly on the right track.

THE POWER OF CBT PIE CHARTS

Ever since I heard this single comment, I knew with absolute certainty that this was going to be the last reflection of the book. Partly because of the Peak-End rule and this is certainly something I want you to remember when you put this book down, but also because I love where this reflection came from.

I think we can all agree here that in our undergraduate psychology lectures it's rare for us to walk anyway from a lecture being amazed by a particular topic. I'm not saying this because I hate psychology, you all know I don't, but I tend to find that even the most amazing topics that I love. They all tend to be a bit boring after two hours.

I think we can all agree on that bit.

Yet what I do find amazing and this is why I love going to lectures, is that every so often you get a simple tangent or one-liner from a lecturer that is truly amazing, inspirational and you remember it.

That's what happened with CBT pie charts and

me.

It was a lecturer with one of my favourite lecturers anyway and whilst I only think I remember the lecture being on trauma, I do remember that she spoke about CBT pie charts as a great way to end psychotherapy.

Since these CBT pie charts are all about making the client realise *they* are the amazing people that have allowed the change to happen and at the end of the day, psychologists are only guides and tool givers. It is the client that has had the power, the will and the determination to change for the better.

What happens in these CBT pie charts as my lecturer explained it is that you get the client to draw a pie chart of how much they think you, as the psychologist, has helped them and how much they have helped themselves. Normally, during this first pie chart the client says something like the psychologist has given me 90% of help and I've only done 10% of the work.

Of course as current or future clinical psychologists, we know this is completely wrong because CBT or whatever psychotherapy you give a person is heavily dependent on them actually engaging in the process and doing it.

All the psychotherapies in the world are useless if a person engages passively, doesn't want to do the work and doesn't want to change.

That's why I use the analogy that clinical psychologists are "merely" tool givers because we only give clients the means and the techniques to change themselves, and create better, more adaptive coping mechanisms for their mental health difficulties.

It is them that actually does something with those tools.

Therefore, with the second pie chart, the therapist starts to gently question and challenge that 90% idea using that analogy or something similar. Then you get the client to realise that they are amazing, they are capable and they are the real reason for the success of the therapy.

In the next pie chart, it is basically a reverse so the client says they've done something around 90% of the work and the therapist has only done 10%.

Of course absolutely none of this is undervaluing or undermining the work of psychologists, because clients could never ever hope to improve and deal with their mental health difficulties without our training, our guidance and our psychological expertise.

Yet as I talk about in one of my introduction to CBT books, when a course of cognitive behavioural therapy, for instance, comes to an end you need to do ending work with the client. Otherwise all the good work done in the therapy can be undone completely if the ending isn't done right.

This is a part of that ending work, and if a client understands that they are the ones in power with their mental health, and they can take that psychology knowledge as well as techniques into the future without the therapist. Then they can understand deeply if they experience mental health difficulties in the future then they are powerful enough to deal with it on their own without the need of a therapist.

Ultimately and hopefully preventing relapse.

And as a profession that's all we actually want. We don't want people to keep having to return to mental health services, we don't want to keep seeing the same client again and again and we certainly don't want them to keep experiencing clinically significant levels of psychological distress.

We need them, want them to improve, not to relapse and go out beyond the therapy room to live a happy, productive life where they aren't in distress because of their difficulties. And if using a CBT pie chart is something that could really help them then this is something we absolutely have to be open to using.

Personally, another reason why I love the idea of CBT pie charts is because at undergraduate-level you don't get to hear about the ins-and-outs of CBT and what techniques are used then. (I know I'm a masters student now but I'm saving those reflections for another reflection book) Therefore, the chance that I had to learn about a specific technique really got me interested.

So as we come to the end of this book, the fourth in the series, about reflecting on the beautiful world of clinical psychology, I have to admit that I am more excited than ever about this profession.

Clinical psychology will never be one thing and that is what keeps it interesting. There will always be new debates, new problems, new therapies to talk about. Just like how there will always be more misconceptions to challenge and there will continue to be new people wanting to come into the profession but face barriers, so we need to tear those barriers down for them.

I love these reflection books because they give me a moment, a time, a chance to express what I think about our profession using fact-based and experience-based opinions that I don't always get to share in other places.

Thank you for joining me in this reflection book and I hope you'll read another psychology book soon, but until then, have a great day.

And always remember to keep being interested, learning and fascinated by the amazing field of clinical psychology.

https://www.subscribepage.com/psychologyboxset

CHECK OUT THE PSYCHOLOGY WORLD PODCAST FOR MORE PSYCHOLOGY INFORMATION! AVAILABLE ON ALL MAJOR PODCAST APPS.

About the author:

Connor Whiteley is the author of over 60 books in the sci-fi fantasy, nonfiction psychology and books for writer's genre and he is a Human Branding Speaker and Consultant.

He is a passionate warhammer 40,000 reader, psychology student and author.

Who narrates his own audiobooks and he hosts The Psychology World Podcast.

All whilst studying Psychology at the University of Kent, England.

Also, he was a former Explorer Scout where he gave a speech to the Maltese President in August 2018 and he attended Prince Charles' 70th Birthday Party at Buckingham Palace in May 2018.

Plus, he is a self-confessed coffee lover!

Other books by Connor Whiteley:
All books in 'An Introductory Series':
Careers In Psychology
Psychology of Suicide
Dementia Psychology
Clinical Psychology Reflections Volume 4
Forensic Psychology of Terrorism And Hostage-Taking
Forensic Psychology of False Allegations
Year In Psychology
CBT For Anxiety
CBT For Depression
Applied Psychology
BIOLOGICAL PSYCHOLOGY 3RD EDITION
COGNITIVE PSYCHOLOGY THIRD EDITION
SOCIAL PSYCHOLOGY- 3RD EDITION
ABNORMAL PSYCHOLOGY 3RD EDITION
PSYCHOLOGY OF RELATIONSHIPS- 3RD EDITION
DEVELOPMENTAL PSYCHOLOGY 3RD EDITION
HEALTH PSYCHOLOGY
RESEARCH IN PSYCHOLOGY
A GUIDE TO MENTAL HEALTH AND

CONNOR WHITELEY

TREATMENT AROUND THE WORLD- A GLOBAL LOOK AT DEPRESSION
FORENSIC PSYCHOLOGY
THE FORENSIC PSYCHOLOGY OF THEFT, BURGLARY AND OTHER CRIMES AGAINST PROPERTY
CRIMINAL PROFILING: A FORENSIC PSYCHOLOGY GUIDE TO FBI PROFILING AND GEOGRAPHICAL AND STATISTICAL PROFILING.
CLINICAL PSYCHOLOGY
FORMULATION IN PSYCHOTHERAPY
PERSONALITY PSYCHOLOGY AND INDIVIDUAL DIFFERENCES
CLINICAL PSYCHOLOGY REFLECTIONS VOLUME 1
CLINICAL PSYCHOLOGY REFLECTIONS VOLUME 2
Clinical Psychology Reflections Volume 3
CULT PSYCHOLOGY
Police Psychology

CLINICAL PSYCHOLOGY REFLECTIONS VOLUME 4

<u>A Psychology Student's Guide To University</u>
How Does University Work?
A Student's Guide To University And Learning
University Mental Health and Mindset

<u>Bettie English Private Eye Series</u>
A Very Private Woman
The Russian Case
A Very Urgent Matter
A Case Most Personal
Trains, Scots and Private Eyes
The Federation Protects
Cops, Robbers and Private Eyes
Just Ask Bettie English
An Inheritance To Die For
The Death of Graham Adams
Bearing Witness
The Twelve
The Wrong Body
The Assassination Of Bettie English

<u>Lord of War Origin Trilogy:</u>
Not Scared Of The Dark
Madness
Burn Them All

The Fireheart Fantasy Series
Heart of Fire
Heart of Lies
Heart of Prophecy
Heart of Bones
Heart of Fate

City of Assassins (Urban Fantasy)
City of Death
City of Marytrs
City of Pleasure
City of Power

Agents of The Emperor
Return of The Ancient Ones
Vigilance
Angels of Fire
Kingmaker
The Eight
The Lost Generation
Hunt
Emperor's Council
Speaker of Treachery
Birth Of The Empire
Terraforma

The Rising Augusta Fantasy Adventure Series
Rise To Power
Rising Walls
Rising Force
Rising Realm

Lord Of War Trilogy (Agents of The Emperor)
Not Scared Of The Dark
Madness
Burn It All Down

Gay Romance Novellas
Breaking, Nursing, Repairing A Broken Heart
Jacob And Daniel
Fallen For A Lie
Spying And Weddings

Miscellaneous:
RETURN
FREEDOM
SALVATION
Reflection of Mount Flame
The Masked One
The Great Deer
English Independence

OTHER SHORT STORIES BY CONNOR WHITELEY

<u>Mystery Short Story Collections</u>

Criminally Good Stories Volume 1: 20 Detective Mystery Short Stories

Criminally Good Stories Volume 2: 20 Private Investigator Short Stories

Criminally Good Stories Volume 3: 20 Crime Fiction Short Stories

Criminally Good Stories Volume 4: 20 Science Fiction and Fantasy Mystery Short Stories

Criminally Good Stories Volume 5: 20 Romantic Suspense Short Stories

<u>Mystery Short Stories:</u>

Protecting The Woman She Hated

Finding A Royal Friend

Our Woman In Paris

Corrupt Driving

A Prime Assassination

Jubilee Thief

Jubilee, Terror, Celebrations

Negative Jubilation

Ghostly Jubilation

Killing For Womenkind

A Snowy Death

Miracle Of Death
A Spy In Rome
The 12:30 To St Pancreas
A Country In Trouble
A Smokey Way To Go
A Spicy Way To GO
A Marketing Way To Go
A Missing Way To Go
A Showering Way To Go
Poison In The Candy Cane
Kendra Detective Mystery Collection Volume 1
Kendra Detective Mystery Collection Volume 2
Mystery Short Story Collection Volume 1
Mystery Short Story Collection Volume 2
Criminal Performance
Candy Detectives
Key To Birth In The Past

<u>Science Fiction Short Stories:</u>
Their Brave New World
Gummy Bear Detective
The Candy Detective
What Candies Fear
The Blurred Image
Shattered Legions

The First Rememberer
Life of A Rememberer
System of Wonder
Lifesaver
Remarkable Way She Died
The Interrogation of Annabella Stormic
Blade of The Emperor
Arbiter's Truth
Computation of Battle
Old One's Wrath
Puppets and Masters
Ship of Plague
Interrogation
Edge of Failure

<u>Fantasy Short Stories:</u>
City of Snow
City of Light
City of Vengeance
Dragons, Goats and Kingdom
Smog The Pathetic Dragon
Don't Go In The Shed
The Tomato Saver
The Remarkable Way She Died
Dragon Coins
Dragon Tea
Dragon Rider

www.ingramcontent.com/pod-product-compliance
Lightning Source LLC
LaVergne TN
LVHW012110070526
838202LV00056B/5685